International Study Centre
Queen Margaret University
Edinburgh EH12 8TS

KU-529-610

FOCUSING ON
IELTS

READING AND WRITING SKILLS

Kerry O'Sullivan
and
Jeremy Lindeck

National Centre for English Language Teaching and Research

Published and distributed by the
National Centre for English Language Teaching and Research
Macquarie University
Sydney NSW 2109

ISBN 1 86408 599 1

MACQUARIE
UNIVERSITY ~ SYDNEY

© Macquarie University 2000

The National Centre for English Language Teaching and Research (NCELTR) is a Commonwealth Government Key Centre of Research and Teaching established at Macquarie University in 1988. The National Centre forms part of the Linguistics discipline at Macquarie University. NCELTR's Key Centre activities are funded by the Commonwealth Department of Immigration and Multicultural Affairs.

Copyright

This book is sold subject to the conditions that it shall not, by way of trade or otherwise, be lent, resold, hired out, or otherwise circulated without the pulisher's prior consent in any form of binding or cover other than that in which it is published and without a similar condition including this condition being imposed on the subsequent purchaser.

All rights reserved. No parts of this publication may be reproduced, stored in a retrieval system, or transmitted, in any form or by any means, electronic, mechanical, photocopying, recording or otherwise, without the prior permission of the publisher.

The publishers have used their best efforts to contact all copyright holders for permission to reproduce artwork and text extracts and wish to acknowledge the following for providing copyright permission.

'Cats – scoundrels or scapegoats?' on page 60 reprinted from the Autumn 1996 issue of Nature Australia by permission of author Tim Low.

The graph on page 99 reprinted from 'Population flows versus immigration aspects', January 1999 by permission of the Department of Immigration and Multicultural Affairs.

The graph on page 127 reprinted from 'Labour market trends' by permission of National Statistics © Crown Copyright 2000.

Descriptions of IELTS sample writing tasks on pages 76, 86–87, 102–103 are reprinted from pages 9–10 of the IELTS handbook January 2000 published in 1999 by permission of the University of Cambridge Local Examinations Syndicate.

Design and DTP: Helen Lavery
Cover design: Peter Vitez
Printed by: Southwood Press Pty Limited

Contents

Acknowledgments

We would like to thank the following people for their professional and personal support throughout the writing of this book:

Liza and Jimmy Lindeck, Martin Sitompul, Graham Taylor, Wattford FC, Louise Melov and Helen Lavery.

We would also like to thank Alison Lyall and Sharon Bennett, IELTS teachers and examiners, for their valuable feedback. We are particularly grateful to Mary Jane Hogan, Senior IELTS Examiner, for her invaluable feedback on content and structure of the book.

Finally we are grateful to Charles College for allowing Jeremy to attend manuscript meetings, and to the University of Cambridge Local Examinations Syndicate for allowing us to reproduce their sample writing tasks.

Kerry O'Sullivan
Jeremy Lindeck

How to use this book

You can use this book individually as an independent-study book to prepare you for the IELTS test or as a coursebook in an IELTS preparation course with a teacher. Most sections of the book are for both General Training (GT) and Academic (A) candidates. Some sections are targeted specifically at General Training candidates or at Academic candidates.

Passages marked **READ ME** give you information about language skills, with **EXAMPLES** to follow and **EXERCISES** for you to do.

You should read and study the book from the beginning to the end. Do Unit 1: Reading first and then Unit 2: Writing.

Both Unit 1: Reading and Unit 2: Writing contain the following six sections.

1   What is in the module?

The first section gives a description of the IELTS test, with information about what it contains, how long it is, what kinds of questions there are, and so on. You should read this section in conjunction with the IELTS Handbook that you receive when you register for the IELTS test.

2   Test-taking tips

The section gives you test-taking tips, advice to help you complete the test within the time allowed and to help you carry out the test in ways that will give you the best mark possible.

3   The strategies you need

The section on strategies gives you advice and some practice on how to read and write as effectively and efficiently as possible when you do the IELTS test.

4   The skills you need

This is the main section of each unit because it explains and practises the skills that you need to do well in the Reading and Writing Modules. These skills include understanding words, understanding what writers are doing, matching information, writing letters, describing and interpreting, and stating points of view. There are a number of short exercises to help you develop these skills. You should do these exercises without assistance and you should follow any time limits suggested. The answers to these exercises are in the Answer Key.

5   Developing your study program

This section helps you develop your own regular self-study program. This involves deciding your needs, finding appropriate practice materials, and practising your skills. There are exercises suggested for individual study and exercises that you can do with a study partner.

6   IELTS practice tests

These practice tests are designed to be similar to the actual IELTS tests for both General Training and Academic candidates. You should do these practice tests without any assistance and you should follow the time limits given.

Summary of exercises

This list gives the aim of each exercise, whether it is for General Training (GT) and/or Academic (A) candidates and where you can find it.

Unit 1: Reading (both General Training and Academic)

Unit 2: Writing (General Training and/or Academic)

Exercise	Focus	Task	GT/A	Page
1	Stating purpose in a letter	1	GT	78
2	Requesting information in a letter	1	GT	80
3	Checking for relevance	1	GT	82
4	Complex sentences	1	GT	84
5	Reading graphs that compare	1	A	90
6	Seeing what writers do in graphs	1	A	91
7	Describing trends	1	A	93
8	Describing trends	1	A	93
9	Describing quantities	1	A	94
10	Describing numbers	1	A	95
11	Comparing graphs	1	A	96
12	Describing a process	1	A	97
13	Describing a process	1	A	98
14	Checking for relevance	1	A	99
15	Describing tables	1	A	100
16	Predicting	2	GT/A	106
17	Arguing	2	GT/A	108
18	Seeing how writers support their viewpoints	2	GT/A	109
19	Seeing how writers support their viewpoints	2	GT/A	110
20	Checking for relevance	2	GT	114
21	Checking for relevance	2	A	115
22	Complex sentences	2	GT/A	117

FOCUSING ON
IELTS

READING
AND
WRITING
SKILLS

UNIT 1: Reading

1 What is in the IELTS reading module?

A comparison of Academic and General Training Reading Modules

		Academic	General training
Reading passages	Different	Three passages from magazines, books, journals or newspapers Topics of general interest At least one passage presents a detailed logical argument	Three passages from notices, advertisements booklets, magazines, timetables, books, journals or newspapers etc Passages focus on social survival, training survival and general reading
Time allowed	Same	60 minutes	60 minutes
Number of questions	Same	40	40
Format of questions	Same	Multiple choice questions Gap-fill questions Short answer questions Matching questions True/False/Not given questions **See examples in 2 Test-taking tips**	Multiple choice questions Gap-fill questions Short answer questions Matching questions True/False/Not given questions **See examples in 2 Test-taking tips**
Test-taking tips	Same	**See in 2 Test-taking tips**	**See in 2 Test-taking tips**

Reading strategies	Same	Skim, scan and read intensively
		
		**See details in
		3 The reading strategies
		  you need**
			Skim, scan and read intensively
			
			**See details in
			3 The reading skills
			  you need**

Reading skills	Same	**See in
		4 The reading skills
		  you need**
			**See in
			4 The reading strategies
			  you need**

Your study program	Same	**See in
		5 Developing your study
		  program**
			**See in
			5 Developing your study
			  program**

READ ME

2 Test-taking tips

What should you do when you take the IELTS reading module?

- Remember what to expect. It is a good idea to look through the whole reading module first, before you start.

- Organise your time while you are doing the test. Even if you have not completed a task in the recommended time, go on to the next task. No question is worth more than a minute.

- Read the questions carefully.

- Try to answer all the questions. If necessary, guess the answer. There are no penalties for wrong answers.

- Try to understand the different question types.

EXAMPLE

To see examples of the question types, read the following passage and answer questions 1 to 12 below.

Life span

A Life span denotes the length of time between conception and death, during which organisms undergo changes in their structure and function.

B All organisms have a finite and species-characteristic life span that reflects the underlying rates of aging. There is a tremendous variation in life span among different groups of organisms.

C Life span is measured either as the maximum age achieved by a member of the species or as an average among the population. The former shows the genetic potential of the species, while the latter, the average life span, is a more meaningful measure.

D In general, organisms live longer in captivity than in the wild. Gender also influences life span, with females usually living 10–15% longer than males in all species.

E The maximum natural life spans of organisms range from about 8 days in some rotifers to over 150 years in tortoises and to 4000 years in certain species of pine trees. Humans are the longest-living mammals and among the longest living of all animals. As of 1985, the highest authenticated age for a human was 120.

Multiple-choice questions

Choose the best answer. Circle **A**, **B**, **C** or **D**.

1 What does 'life span' mean?

   A how long organisms live

   B how organisms change

   C the variation among organisms

   D life in captivity

… continued over

… continued

2 How many ways of measuring 'life span' are there?

    A three

    B several

    C two

    D many

Gap-filling questions

Complete the summary by choosing words from the list.

conception   length   time   organisms   changes   function

'Life span', a concept which can be applied to all … (**3**) …, is calculated not from the birth of the organism, but rather from its … (**4**) …

Complete the notes below. Use NO MORE THAN TWO WORDS for each answer.

- *life span = time between conception/death*
- *different organisms have different spans*
- *measure … (**5**) … age or average age*
- *life span in captivity > in wild*
- *life span … (**6**) … > males*
- *range = 8 days to 4000 years*
- *oldest person = 120*

Short-answer questions

Answer the following questions. Write NO MORE THAN THREE WORDS for each answer.

7 How old was the longest living person? _____

8 What is the longest life span ever recorded? _____

9 Which gender lives longer? _____

Matching questions

The reading passage has five paragraphs labelled A to E.
Which paragraphs contain the following information?

10 Examples of life spans in different organisms _____

11 A definition of 'life span' _____

12 A description of ways of calculating 'life span' _____

Note: The answers to questions 1 to 12 are given in the Answer Key.

3 The reading strategies you need

How should you read? The IELTS test requires you to read effectively and efficiently. Being an effective and efficient reader means more than knowing what each word in the passage means.

READ ME

Let's check the basic strategy. When you start to read a passage you need to ask yourself these three questions:

What am I reading?

Why am I reading it?

How am I going to read it?

EXAMPLE

Look at the examples in the table.

What?	Why?	How?
A letter from a friend	For pleasure/ information	READ the letter INTENSIVELY, that is, read it from the first word to the last word.
A magazine	For pleasure/ information	SKIM the magazine, that is, glance at the headings and photos. If an article seems interesting, read more until you finish the article or you lose interest. Move on to the next heading or photo.
An airline ticket	For information, eg the flight number	SCAN the ticket, that is, look over it quickly until you find the information you need. Ignore the other information.

Successful candidates use all three ways of reading.

> **What successful candidates do**
>
> - SKIM the passage to get a general understanding of the main points in the passage.
> - SCAN the passage to locate the specific information needed to answer a question.
> - READ this information INTENSIVELY to decide on the answer.

In the IELTS test, use this three-step strategy for reading as described below.

STEP 1: SKIMMING

READ ME

Skim the passage so that you have a general understanding of the main points in it.

When you are skimming a passage for a general understanding, don't try to understand every word. Jump from paragraph to paragraph, finding the main point in each paragraph before moving on to the next paragraph, like jumping across stepping-stones in a river. The main point of each paragraph is often, though certainly not always, the first sentence in each paragraph. The sentence with the main point is often called the 'topic sentence'. Taken together, the topic sentences of a passage should provide a reasonable summary of the passage.

When you are looking at sentences to understand the main points, try to find the main words in the sentence, namely the subject, the verb and the object of the main clause. Try to ignore the other words, particularly the relative clauses and adverbial clauses. Say, for example, you are skimming through the following sentence in a passage:

EXAMPLE

Whale oil, rendered from the blubber, was used originally for lamp fuel and later as a principal ingredient of soaps, margarine, paint oils and lubricants.

While skimming, it is enough to understand that: (This) oil was used for (something). Or, say you are skimming this sentence:

Tea plants are grown on tea plantations, called gardens or estates, in areas that have a great amount of rainfall and rich loamy soil.

It is enough to understand that tea plants are grown on/in somewhere/somehow. If you later find a question that relates to this sentence, you can come back and read it more intensively.

READ ME

When you have finished skimming the passage, skim the questions. You need to know how many questions there are and approximately what the questions are about. You can now practise skimming. To encourage you to skim as quickly as possible, there is a suggested time limit.

Exercise 1: Skimming

Skim the following passage as quickly as possible and underline the sentence that gives the main point of each paragraph.

Time limit: 1 minute

Libraries

Libraries are quite difficult to define. If you ask most people to define a library, they will probably say that it is a building with a lot of books. Strictly speaking, a library does not have to be a building: it can be a room, or indeed any area where material is kept. Equally, a library is not merely a collection of books: there are journals, newspapers, CD-ROMs, microfilm, audio-visual materials and so on. So, to be more accurate we can say that a library is a collection of information or material.

Libraries are organised in three ways. Most libraries will use one or more of the three main classification systems that have been developed to detail the material in the collection. They are referred to as the Dewey Decimal System, the Universal Decimal Classification and the Library of Congress System.

Nowadays libraries are under threat for a number of reasons. The primary challenge, as never before, is funding. Hardware and personnel costs increase each time technology expands. Equally, there are challenges in the skills needed by users and resource professionals.

It is difficult to predict the future of libraries. Our basic concept of libraries will almost certainly, it would appear, change dramatically in that we will not think of them (and access them) as physical places, which is the prevailing concept at the moment. But beyond that, it is difficult to predict both usage patterns and preferred systems of data recording and retrieval.

STEP 2: SCANNING

Scan the passage to locate the specific information you need to answer each question.

When you are scanning to locate some specific information, it is not necessary to read and understand every word in the passage. When you look at each sentence, you need to understand only enough to answer the question: *Is this what I am looking for or not?* So, you only need to understand the topic of each sentence. Let's say you are doing the IELTS test and you are trying to answer a question about shoes. You scan the passage to find the information that will give you the answer. You look at each sentence very quickly. For example, you see this sentence:

EXAMPLE Like perfumes, *cosmetics* were originally used as an adjunct to religious ritual, the ceremonial aspects gradually being lost as both men and women adorned themselves with cosmetics.

You locate the subject of the sentence 'cosmetics' and that is enough. It is not necessary to read all the details. You know that this sentence probably does not contain the information you need, so you quickly move on to the next sentence. This is scanning. It is similar to skimming in that you need to jump from sentence to sentence, and paragraph to paragraph. You can now practise scanning. To encourage you to scan as quickly as possible, there is a suggested time limit.

Exercise 2: Scanning

Scan the passage about libraries. Which sentence contains the information you need to answer the questions below? Write the number of the sentence from the passage next to each question. **Time limit: 2 minutes**

(1) Libraries are quite difficult to define. (2) If you ask most people to define a library, they will probably say that it is a building with a lot of books. (3) Strictly speaking, a library does not have to be a building: it can be a room, or indeed any area where material is kept. (4) Equally, a library is not merely a collection of books: there are journals, newspapers, CD-ROMs, microfilm, audio-visual materials and so on. (5) So, to be more accurate we can say that a library is a collection of information or material.

(6) Libraries are organised in three ways. (7) Most libraries will use one or more of the three main classification systems that have been developed to detail the material in the collection. (8) They are referred to as the Dewey Decimal System, the Universal Decimal Classification and the Library of Congress System.

(9) Nowadays libraries are under threat for a number of reasons. (10) The primary challenge, as never before, is funding. (11) Hardware and personnel costs increase each time technology expands. (12) Equally, there are challenges in the skills needed by users and resource professionals.

(13) It is difficult to predict the future of libraries. (14) Our basic concept of libraries will almost certainly, it would appear, change dramatically in that we will not think of them (and access them) as physical places, which is the prevailing concept at the moment. (15) But beyond that, it is difficult to predict both usage patterns and preferred systems of data recording and retrieval. ... continued over

... continued

1	What kinds of materials does a library collect?	_____4_____
2	What is the most accurate way to define 'library'?	_____
3	What is the main problem that libraries are facing?	_____
4	What aspect of libraries is sure to change?	_____

STEP 3: READING INTENSIVELY

READ ME   Read one section of the passage carefully to understand what is needed to answer the question.

After you have scanned and located your information, you must read those sentences intensively. Reading intensively is different from skimming and scanning. When you skim and scan you only need to understand some key words: the subject, verb and object. Now it may be necessary to understand every word.

You can now practise reading intensively. To encourage you to read as quickly as possible, there is a suggested time limit.

Exercise 3: Reading intensively

Answer the questions below. Scan the passage about libraries to locate the sentences that contain the answers. Then read the sentences intensively. Use NO MORE THAN FOUR WORDS in each answer.   **Time limit: 2 minutes**

1   What is ONE type of material that libraries collect, beside books? _____

2   How many types of classification systems are there?   _____

3   What kinds of costs increase when technologies expand?   _____

4   How do most people conceptualise libraries?   _____

Now practise the three-step reading strategy in Exercises 4 to 6. Be careful to follow the suggested time limits.

Remember – follow this three-step reading strategy

- SKIM the passage and the questions to get a quick general understanding.
- SCAN the passage to locate the information you need to answer each question.
- READ this information INTENSIVELY so that you can answer the questions.

Exercise 4: Reading strategies

Read the following passage and answer the questions below. Use NO MORE THAN FOUR WORDS in each answer.   **Time limit: 3 minutes**

Esperanto

Esperanto is an artificial language designed to serve internationally as an auxiliary means of communication among speakers of different languages. Esperanto, the creation of Ludwig Zamenhof, a Polish–Jewish ophthalmologist, was first presented in 1887. An international movement to promote its use has continued to flourish and has members in more than 80 countries.

Esperanto is used internationally across language boundaries by about one million people, particularly in specialised fields. It is used in personal contacts, on radio broadcasts, and in a number of publications as well as in translations of both modern works and classics. Its popularity has spread from Europe – both East and West – to such countries as Brazil and Japan. It is in China, however, that Esperanto has had its greatest impact. It is taught in universities and used in many translations (often in scientific or technological works). *El Popola Cinio*, a monthly magazine in Esperanto from the People's Republic of China, is read worldwide. Radio Beijing's Esperanto program is the most popular program in Esperanto in the world.

Esperanto's vocabulary is drawn primarily from Latin, the Romance languages, English and German. Spelling is completely regular. A simple and consistent set of endings indicates grammatical functions of words. Thus, for example, every noun ends in -o, every adjective in -a, and the infinitive of every verb in -i.

1 Who created Esperanto? _____Ludwig Zamenhof_____

2 When was Esperanto created? _____

3 How many people use Esperanto? _____

4 Name TWO countries where Esperanto is used. _____

5 In which country is Esperanto taught at universities? _____

6 Does Esperanto vocabulary come from eastern or western languages? _____

7 What kinds of words end in -a in Esperanto? _____

Exercise 5: Reading strategies

Read the following passage and then choose the best answer. Circle **A**, **B**, **C** or **D**.

Time limit: 3 minutes

Migrant labour

Migrant workers, those workers who move repeatedly in search of economic opportunity, typically perform society's temporary jobs. The migrant's low-paid work includes 'stooped labour' like cultivating crops, menial services such as cleaning public rest rooms, 'sweatshop' work such as making apparel, and assembly-line factory work like putting together computer parts. Migrant workers are often pivotal for economic growth.

Until the twentieth century most migrant labour was internal. For example, generations of former slaves from the southern parts of the United States annually followed the crops north. Recently, however, most migrant labour in Europe and America has been external – that is, workers from other countries.

Migrant workers rarely understand the customs and language of their host societies and are frequently ill-housed, malnourished, underpaid, and denied basic legal rights. Their children fall behind in school and are then apt to be put to work in violation of child labour laws. Poor sanitation, unsafe drinking water and overcrowded living conditions make migrant labourers especially susceptible to contagious disease. In the 1980s and 1990s their tuberculosis and hepatitis rates far exceeded national norms. AIDS also spread rapidly. In short, the lives of migrant workers tend to be less comfortable and shorter than those of non-migrants.

International economics determines where external migrants go. In the 1940s, when railroad workers and farmhands went off to fight in World War II, the United States reached an agreement with Mexico to provide millions of temporary Mexican migrants. In the postwar period, 'guest workers' from southern Europe, Turkey and North Africa helped rebuild north-western Europe. In the 1970s and 1980s the oil-rich monarchs of Saudi Arabia and Kuwait flew Asians in to build their new cities.

1   Cultivating crops is an example of …

   A   economic growth.

   B   stooped labour.

   C   a typical job.

   D   factory work.

2   Migrant workers usually speak the language of their host society …

   A   very fluently.

   B   very poorly.

   C   as well as their first language.

   D   quite well.

3   The flow of migrant workers generally relates to …

   A   war.

   B   labor laws.

   C   legal rights.

   D   economic needs.

Are the statements below *True*, *False* or *Not given* according to the passage? Circle T, F or NG. The first has been done for you.   **Time limit: 3 minutes**

Rice

Since ancient times, rice has been the most commonly used food grain for the majority of people in the world. A member of the grass family Graminae, rice (*Oryza sativa*) can be grown successfully under climatic conditions ranging from tropical to temperate. Properly cultivated, rice produces higher yields than any other grain with the exception of corn, and although the total area planted in rice is far smaller than that devoted to wheat (the world total is about one-third less), the rice crop feeds a far greater proportion of the world's population.

In contrast to wheat and corn, only a small percentage of the total rice crop enters international trade. Not quite 4% of the total worldwide becomes an export commodity, although the United States exports approximately 45% of its total production. Limited international trade in rice has prevented the establishment of large, active trading centres like those for marketing cereal grains, and formulation of official grain standards for rice has been slow to develop.

During the past quarter of a century, rice-breeding programs have been initiated in several countries. Resistance to diseases and insects was the major objective of the earlier research, but hybrid programs have dominated recently. High-yielding dwarf plants that can withstand deep water and that respond to fertilisers have been developed. Improved grain quality and higher protein levels have been added objectives of new programs designed to improve nutrition.

1	Rice has been eaten since ancient times.	(T)	F	NG
2	Rice is a member of the grass family.	T	F	NG
3	Rice can only be grown in tropical climates.	T	F	NG
4	Some people eat rice three times a day.	T	F	NG
5	Rice feeds more people than wheat.	T	F	NG
6	Most rice is traded internationally.	T	F	NG
7	Thailand is a major exporter of rice.	T	F	NG
8	Rice breeding programs are concentrated in one country.	T	F	NG

READ ME   From now on, remember to skim, scan and read intensively as appropriate when you do the practice exercises, when you take the IELTS reading module and when you read at university or college or generally.

4 The reading skills you need

There are three main skills that will help you when you read generally and when you do the IELTS reading module: understanding the words; understanding what writers are doing; and matching information when you read.

READ ME

UNDERSTANDING THE WORDS

When you skim and scan it is not necessary to understand every word in the passage. Usually, however, you must know over 50% of the words if you want to understand the main points of the passage.

You should immediately begin a program of vocabulary development and aim to learn five to ten new words a day. You can do this by reading as much as possible. Choose articles that you find interesting in newspapers, magazines, encyclopedias and textbooks.

Expanding your vocabulary is important not only for your reading, but also for your writing, speaking and listening.

Choosing useful words to learn

Which words should you learn? You cannot and should not try to learn every word. Instead, you need to learn the most useful words, that is, those words that can be used in a wide range of passages. On the other hand, 'technical' words have very limited use as they are usually used in one field only.

Look at the following example taken from a newspaper article. Words that you might find useful to learn have been underlined. Technical terms are in *italics*.

EXAMPLE

> Goran Ivanisevic <u>fears</u> only one *service* in tennis – Michael Stich's. 'His *toss* is always the <u>same</u>, the <u>straight</u> one or the *topspin*. Sampras has a good *serve* and Becker too, but Stich's is the <u>toughest</u> to <u>read</u>.'

The underlined words can be used when talking about other topics, not just tennis, but the words in italics are often used only in tennis and so are less useful to you.

Exercise 7: Selecting vocabulary to learn

Read the following paragraph taken from a textbook. Underline the words you think might be useful to learn. Then check all your underlined words in a dictionary.

An inspection of the skin can reveal alterations such as extreme dryness, growths, ulcers and discolouration. The breasts, prostate and genitals are palpated to detect tumours, and endoscopic examination of the rectum and colon may be appropriate in older persons.

Exercise 8: Selecting vocabulary to learn

Read the following paragraph taken from a textbook. Underline the words you think might be useful to learn. Then check all your underlined words in a dictionary.

How do we humans produce speech? First the brain issues a command to the lungs to initiate an airstream. Before this airstream can become speech, however, it must pass through, or by, the larynx, pharynx, tongue, teeth, lips and nose – all of which can modify the airstream in various ways.

If there are difficult technical words in the IELTS passages, you will be given their meanings in a glossary, that is, a mini-dictionary at the end of the passage.

Learning useful words

There are different ways of learning new words. Keep experimenting to decide which approaches are the most successful for you. Write the words down. Write the words again and again. Say the new words aloud many times. Create your own dictionary with all your new words. You could arrange them alphabetically or functionally. If you arranged them functionally you might, for example, use the heading 'words associated with the office', 'words that help you compare' or 'words associated with university'. Create a simple example to help you remember the new word. For example, if you want to remember the word 'various', you could write an easy sentence to illustrate the meaning of the word, for example: *You can cook eggs in various ways*.

When you were studying English at high school and university you probably wanted to understand every word of the passages you read – and perhaps you wrote the translation above each new word. As you now move towards doing the IELTS test and studying courses in English, you will need to change this approach. It is not possible or realistic to know the precise meaning of every word you see. Sometimes it is necessary to accept an approximate meaning of words. It would be better, for example, to know the approximate meaning of 2000 words than the precise meaning of 1000 words.

Here is a summary of strategies for learning new vocabulary.

Useful strategies	Not-so-useful strategies
Only look up those words you think might be very useful. Don't try to learn/remember every new word.	Look up every new word in a (bilingual) dictionary.
Use an English-English dictionary (maybe the Australian Learners Dictionary). Even if you don't understand the precise meaning of the word, you are expanding your vocabulary and using good reading strategies.	Try to remember every new word you find.

As you develop your vocabulary, you will probably know the vast majority of the words in the reading passages. But you will not know every word in every passage. Faced with unknown words, some readers panic and believe they will not be able to answer the questions. Remember, however, that you often do not need to understand every word to carry out the required tasks. Also, you can often guess the meaning of an unknown word, especially if you can see what the writer is doing.

For example, look at this exercise. Read the paragraph about obesity and answer the questions.

> Obesity is a medical disorder that affects approximately 20–30% of the population of the United States of America. It is an excessive accumulation of body fat that results from the storage of excess food energy calories in the body's fat cells.
>
> **1** Most American people suffer from obesity. True, False or Not given?
>
> **2** This paragraph presents …
>
> **A** some examples of obesity.
>
> **B** a definition of obesity.
>
> **C** the different types of obesity.
>
> **D** the treatment of obesity.

When reading this paragraph, a student found many unknown words and underlined them. However, both questions can be answered (**1** False; **2** B) without knowing the meaning of the underlined words. It is not even necessary to understand the word 'obesity'!

If it does seem necessary to understand the meaning of a particular unfamiliar word, you will have to guess. One way of guessing is to look at the relationship of that word to other nearby words. Using general knowledge also helps in guessing the meaning of unknown words. Guess the meaning of 'obesity' and then check a dictionary to see if your guess was right.

Guessing: A useful strategy

Read this sentence from a passage about computer crime.

> Computers have been used for most kinds of crime, including fraud, theft, larceny, embezzlement, burglary, sabotage, espionage, murder and forgery, since the first cases were reported in 1958.

You come to the word 'fraud' and realise that you don't know this word. You immediately move to the next word and see that this word is also unfamiliar. You stay calm and move on. There are many words you don't know but you move on. Later, you find one of these two things:

- There are no questions relating to this sentence. You don't have to understand this sentence to answer the questions.

- There is a question relating to this sentence. So, you go back to the sentence and focus on the words you do know. For example, imagine you know all the following words in the paragraph:

> Computers have been used for most kinds of crime, including __, __, __, __, __, __, __, murder and __, since the first cases were reported in 1958.

You can see that the sentence is presenting examples of kinds of computer crime. Using your general knowledge, you guess that the unknown words are types of crime such as stealing money or stealing information. That is enough for you to be able to answer the question.

READ ME Guessing is an important strategy when reading at university or college and in the IELTS reading module. Try this strategy in the following exercises: Skim the passage quickly. If there are words you don't know, don't stop and don't panic. Keep moving forward. Look at each question after the passage. If there are questions that relate to the words that you don't understand, look at the nearby words and sentences and then guess the meaning of the unknown words.

Now practise your reading strategies in Exercises 9 and 10.

Remember – follow this three-step reading strategy

- SKIM the passage and the questions to get a quick general understanding.
- SCAN the passage to locate the information you need to answer each question.
- READ this information INTENSIVELY so that you can answer the questions.

Exercise 9: Reading strategies

Read the paragraph about obesity and answer the questions.

Obesity results from an imbalance of the body's food intake, physical activity and resting metabolism. A variety of both psychological and physiological factors play a role. Certain endocrine gland disorders, such as hypothyroidism or tumours of the adrenal gland, pancreas or pituitary gland, may cause obesity. Recent research has found that a reduction of the body's resting metabolic rate also has a significant effect on the development of obesity. However, most obesity results from using food excessively as an inappropriate coping mechanism to deal with emotional stress.

1 Obesity results from psychological factors only. True, False or Not given?

2 This paragraph presents …

   A the causes of obesity.

   B the impact of obesity.

   C the solutions to obesity.

   D the different types of obesity.

3 What do the following words mean?

   A obesity _____

   B reduction _____

   C excessively _____

Exercise 10: Reading strategies

Read the paragraph about the ozone layer and answer the questions.

The ozone layer is a layer of the upper atmosphere about 20 to 25 km above the earth's surface. It is so named because the unstable form of oxygen called ozone is concentrated in this layer. The ozone layer strongly absorbs ultraviolet radiation from the sun. If this radiation reached the earth's surface at unprotected levels, it would be deleterious to all forms of life. For example, it would raise the incidence of human skin cancers and cataracts, as well as reducing food production in general.

1 Ozone is a form of oxygen. True, False or Not given?

2 This paragraph presents

    A a general description of the ozone layer.

    B an account of a recent problem involving the ozone layer.

    C a recommendation of how to solve the ozone problem.

    D a classification of the different types of oxygen.

3 What do the following words mean?

    A deleterious _____

    B incidence _____

UNDERSTANDING WHAT WRITERS ARE DOING

READ ME

If you are able to see what writers are doing, it will be easier to understand what they are saying. This will help you with your reading at university or college and also with the IELTS test.

Learning to see what writers are doing will help you do the following question types in the reading module: classifying; presenting arguments; choosing from a list of headings; reading graphs, tables and illustrations; and reading notes, summaries, diagrams, flow charts and tables.

Broadly speaking, writers do the following:

1 **Writers describe.** They present information. They describe processes. They describe what happened. They define and label things. They classify things into different types. This kind of writing is called 'descriptive writing'. A manual for a microwave oven, a library catalogue, a news article about a car accident, a children's story and a laboratory report are all examples of descriptive texts.

2 **Writers argue.** They give opinions. They express their viewpoints. They make claims. They give reasons. They give evidence to support their claims. They predict what will happen. This is called 'argumentative writing'. A letter to the editor of a newspaper, a newspaper editorial, a political pamphlet, and a university essay about the advantages and disadvantages of using computers are all examples of argumentative texts.

Of course many pieces of writing include examples of both describing and arguing.

Reading descriptive texts

When you read descriptive texts, you need to be able to read definitions, labels, classifications and descriptions of processes.

Reading definitions

EXAMPLE   Read some sample definitions.

Inflation is a process in which the average level of prices increases at a substantial rate over a considerable period of time.

The writer is defining 'inflation'. One common way of defining is to say that 'this person/thing is a (noun) who/that (clause)'. Look at the following definitions.

A calculator is a machine that performs mathematical operations.

Chess is a game for two people that is played on a square board of eight rows of eight squares each, alternately light and dark in colour.

A dictionary is a list of words and phrases that are arranged alphabetically and give the pronunciation, alternate spelling and meaning of each entry.

Genetics is the science that studies all aspects of inherited characteristics.

Stock markets are associations of brokers and dealers in securities who transact business together.

The lemming is a rodent that is closely related to the vole and the meadow mouse.

Tea is the beverage that is made when the processed leaves of the tea plant are infused with boiling water.

When you know what the writer is doing, you have a better chance of understanding individual words. For example, now that you know that the writer is defining tea in the example above, what do you think the word 'beverage' means? Is this a new word for you? You can now see that it is possible to work out the meaning of words if you know what a writer is doing. Similarly, in the definition of 'lemming', you only need to know the word 'mouse' to work out that a lemming is a kind of animal related to the mouse.

Exercise 11: Defining

Define the following words.

A   library   A library is a   _____

B   refrigerator   A refrigerator is a   _____

C   widow   A widow is a   _____

D   fax machine   A fax machine is a   _____

Reading labels

In the sentence below the writer is labelling something, that is, giving the roof of the mouth an appropriate name, the 'velum'.

> These are sounds formed by pushing the tongue against the back of the roof of the mouth, <u>called</u> the velum.

Read some more examples of sentences in which the writer is labelling.

EXAMPLE

> This type of tree <u>is called</u> a banksia.

> These sounds are formed by pushing the tongue against the back of the roof of the mouth, <u>known as</u> the velum.

> He is a polyglot, <u>that is</u>, a person who speaks many languages.

> A <u>so-called</u> phonetic transcription, a series of letters enclosed in square brackets to indicate pronunciation, can provide no more than a rough visible record of the succession of noises that is human speech.

> Certain acquired disorders involve the '<u>pericardium</u>', two thin layers that surround the heart, or the '<u>myocardium</u>', the muscular tissue of the heart.

Sometimes writers will show you that a word is a label by using inverted commas, for example, 'pericardium'. If it is a technical label or a foreign word, they may use italics. The last example above presents two labels, 'pericardium' and 'myocardium'. Note that in each case the label and the explanation are simply placed side by side. Here are two more examples of labelling in this way.

> His main hobby is philately, the collecting of stamps.

> The jackfruit, a large tropical fruit, is grown widely in this region.

When people read every word rather than skimming and scanning first, they may not see that the meaning of a difficult word is often right next door!

Exercise 12: Reading labels

Read the sentences and answer the following questions.

1 One form of transport that is very popular with tourists is the 'tuk-tuk', a motorised three-wheeled vehicle.

What is a tuk-tuk? _____

2 This feeling of strangeness and discomfort, or 'culture shock' as it is usually called, can result in quite severe distress.

What is culture shock? _____

3 He is a polyglot, that is, a person who speaks many languages.

What is a polyglot? _____

4 One of the most devastating social events of the twentieth century was the period of economic collapse in the late 1920s and early 1930s, the so-called Great Depression.

What was the Great Depression? _____

… continued over

... continued

5 The plant selected for landscaping the forecourt of the building was the leptospermum, an attractive, low-growing tea-tree suited to garden beds or containers.

What is a leptospermum? _____

6 During the 1800s several pesticides, chemical agents used to control pests, were discovered and widely employed. Paris green, for instance, was accidentally found to control leaf-eating insects. Bordeaux mixture, a complex of copper sulfate and hydrated lime in water, came into use as a preventive fungicide and insect repellent.

A What do you call chemical agents that are used to control pests? _____

B What is 'Paris green'? _____

C What do you call a complex of copper sulfate and hydrated lime in water? _____

Reading classifications

Here is an example of a sentence that classifies.

EXAMPLE

When considering word order, that is, the relative sequence of subject (S), verb (V) and object (O) in a sentence, <u>there are three main types of</u> languages in the world: SOV, SVO (of which English is an example) and VSO.

This writer is classifying the languages of the world into different types or categories. Here are two other examples of classification.

The problems <u>can be divided</u> into three types: personnel problems, systems problems and logistical issues.

<u>There are five distinct species of</u> this plant found throughout the highland regions, each with different environmental adaptations.

Exercise 13: Reading classifications

Read the following paragraph and complete 1 to 3 in the table below.

There are only three main kinds of tea: black tea, which is fermented, green tea, which is unfermented, and oolong tea, which is semi-fermented. Black tea is predominant in Western countries while green tea and oolong are particularly popular in East Asia.

	Tea	
1...	unfermented	East Asia
2...	semi-fermented	East Asia
3...	fermented	Western countries

Exercise 14: Reading classifications

Read the following paragraph and complete 1 to 3 in the table below.

In this lowest-income category, employment is usually divided into three types: so-called stooped labour such as cultivating crops, sweatshop work such as making clothing, and assembly-line work like assembling computer parts. All three types of employment have increased their share of total employment in this district during the period surveyed (1996–1999), with assembly-line work showing the greatest continual increase. Stooped labour seems to have slowed, registering no change in the past two years.

Employment type	Share of total employment, Camba District, 1996–1999			
	1996	**1997**	**1998**	**1999**
1	0%	58%	59%	59%
2	30%	49%	68%	89%
3	24%	26%	31%	38%

Reading processes

When writers describe processes, they are describing a number of steps in a particular sequence – the right steps in the right order.

EXAMPLE The following is an example of a writer describing a process or sequence. In other words, the writer is giving instructions (in this case, how to open a notebook computer).

1 Unlatch the two clasps located along the sides of the top cover.

2 Lift the top cover to reveal the display panel, keyboard and system controls.

3 Raise the display panel to a comfortable viewing angle.

Here are other examples of writers describing a process or giving instructions.

<u>First</u>, click on 'format', <u>then</u> 'autoformat' and <u>then</u> 'options. Select 'auto-correct' and follow the directions it contains.

The harvested grain is <u>first</u> washed and <u>then</u> dried <u>before</u> being ground.

<u>After</u> the ballot papers are collected, they are keyed into a computer <u>and</u> <u>then</u> checked by a supervisor <u>before</u> being filed.

Exercise 15: Reading processes

Read the following passage. Choose the summary (**A**, **B** or **C**) that accurately presents the process described in the passage.

After you have planned the unit of materials you are going to produce, give your unit a title and determine its location. Key in the unit and module headings, and select one of the modules to begin developing. Now you have to import your media file. Once you have the film in place, you must then produce (or import) the transcript. Make sure your transcript is accurate before you go on to the next step. It is not very convenient to have to come back later to adjust the transcript. With the transcript completed, the next step is to 'smart-link' the transcript to the film. When this is completed, you are ready to start writing exercises.

Summary A	Summary B	Summary C
plan unit	plan unit	fix title/location
fix title/location	fix title/location	plan unit
key in headings	key in headings	key in headings
transcript	import media file	import media file
import media file	transcript	transcript
smart-link	check transcript	smart-link
check transcript	smart-link	check transcript
write exercises	write exercises	write exercises

Reading argumentative texts

READ ME

When writers argue they put forward their own opinions. They say things like: 'This is better than that', 'That problem was caused by this', 'This will change' and 'I think we should do this'.

Presenting your opinions is a fundamental way of writing at university or college. You must be able to read this kind of 'argumentative' writing. At least one passage in the Academic Reading Module contains detailed logical argument. The General Training Reading Module may also contain an argumentative text.

In a piece of argumentative writing, you will usually see that:

- There is an issue (a question, a problem). Writers put forward their own viewpoints about this issue. They make claims (they say they have the answers). They put forward an argument or 'case'. They draw implications. They anticipate what will happen (they speculate).

- They put forward evidence to support their claim. This is an important point in university study. You need to be able to see whether you are reading the writer's subjective opinion or a fact supported by objective evidence. Writers argue against someone else's claims. They oppose other viewpoints.

When you read argumentative texts, you need to be able to judge the writer's viewpoint, read comparisons and contrasts, examples and reasons.

Exercise 16: Reading argumentative texts

Read the following passage and answer the questions. The sentences are numbered 1 to 4.

(1) Who is at fault in the unfortunate incident of last Wednesday where demonstrators outside Government House clashed so violently with security guards? (2) Some have suggested that the security guards were to blame for using dogs, but surely the use of dogs is perfectly standard nowadays, and should not draw criticism. (3) The photographs published yesterday of the injuries to the dogs shows that the situation is not as straightforward as we first thought. (4) Clearly, the demonstrators must take a good part of the blame themselves.

1 In which sentence does the writer state the issue? _____

2 In which sentence does the writer give his/her opinion about who is at fault? _____

3 In which sentence does the writer argue against someone else's claim? _____

Exercise 17: Reading argumentative texts

Read the following passage and then choose the best answer. Circle **A**, **B** or **C**.

Genetically-modified organisms (GMOs) are a double-edged sword. While they can help reduce farm production costs, they may cause harmful effects as well. Controversy has erupted that genetically-modified cotton has been widely planted in the current season. A committee appointed by the government to assess the safety of the cotton has yet to conclude its findings. We should not rush to conclude that genetically-modified cotton is totally safe, as some members of the committee have done, or say that it is dangerous, as some non-governmental organisations have claimed.

Research into genetically-modified crops should be encouraged. But we must realise that it is a double-edged sword. We are not blindly against GMOs. But everyone must come clean in this matter. GM crops that are resistant to pests and provide better yields should be developed. But steps must be taken to ensure that they will not create disastrous side effects for the people and the environment.

1 What is the writer's viewpoint about the development of GMOs?

  A She strongly supports it because of its benefits.

  B She opposes it because of the disastrous side effects.

  C She argues that we should be aware of both the benefits and side effects.

2 The writer argues that we should …

  A not believe the claims of some committee members.

  B not accept the views of some non-governmental organisations.

  C be careful about the claims of all parties involved.

3 What would be a good title for this passage?

  A GM crops must be studied

  B Stop GM crops now

  C GM crops the hope of the future

Judging the writer's viewpoint

READ ME

When studying at university or college it is often not enough to understand what you read – you must be able to evaluate it as well. Often this evaluation requires you to decide the writer's point of view.

To decide a writer's viewpoint about an issue, you must locate evidence, judge the evidence and make a decision. For example, in the passage about GMOs in Exercise 17, is the writer in favour of or opposed to GMOs? The following evidence can be found in the passage:

For Does the writer support GMOs?	**Against** Does the writer oppose GMOs?
• They can help reduce farm production costs. • We should not say that it is dangerous. • GM crops that are resistant to pests and provide better yields should be developed. • We are not blindly against GMOs.	• They may cause harmful effects. • We should not rush to conclude that genetically-modified cotton is perfectly safe.

There is evidence both for and against GMOs. The writer accepts possible benefits and also acknowledges possible risks. We can say, therefore, that the writer's viewpoint is that she neither supports nor opposes GMOs. Her stance or position on this issue is neutral. This conclusion is supported by the writer's statement that GMOs are a 'double-edged sword' – something which brings both benefits and problems.

Apart from locating and judging the evidence, you need to pay attention to the words that the writer chooses. This can also show the writer's viewpoint and attitude.

EXAMPLE

For example, the two passages below present more or less the same factual information, but their writers appear to have different viewpoints.

A Christian churches have had an important impact on this country since the arrival of the first missionaries in 1733. The majority of people (perhaps as many as 98% by some accounts) are now members of established Christian churches. All the churches play a significant role through their missions in providing health and education services in the country. Nevertheless, traditional religion still plays an important part in society, and many people, particularly in rural areas, retain beliefs in traditional spirits.

B Since Christian missionaries first swarmed ashore in 1733, their churches have exercised a truly enormous influence on this country. The majority of people (some claims put forward are as high as 98%) now line up as members of established Christian churches. All the churches play a significant role in society, with their missions deeply entrenched in health and education. Nevertheless, traditional religion still plays an important part in society, and many people, particularly in rural areas, draw comfort from their devotion to traditional spirits.

The language in passage B is more emotional than in passage A. It appears that the writer of passage B is more negative towards the missionaries and churches and more positive towards the traditional beliefs. Look at the following phrases from the passages that present the same information but in different ways.

A: *the arrival of the first missionaries*

B: *missionaries first swarmed ashore*

Both phrases are about the arrival of the missionaries but in passage B the missionaries are described as 'swarming' ashore. The word 'swarm' is usually used in relation to large numbers of insects; for example, bees swarm. The writer wants to give the impression that the missionaries were like swarming insects. In doing so, the writer is being negative in her description of the arrival of the missionaries.

A: *providing health and education*

B: *deeply entrenched in health and education*

The word 'entrenched' says more than 'provides': it implies that the missionaries are deeply involved and are difficult to remove. It has a more negative meaning.

A: *retain beliefs*

B: *draw comfort from their devotion*

The writer in phrase A simply states that they have kept their religion while the writer in phrase B implies that this brings a positive benefit. The second version is more positive.

Exercise 18: Judging a writer's viewpoint

Read the passage below and answer the questions.

Care needs to be taken with religious items. There have been a number of incidents over the years involving foreigners that have drawn a strong reaction from an offended government and people – for example, the family of tourists who foolishly clambered all over a revered Buddha statue. When buying an object, it is important to distinguish between the object's aesthetic appeal and its religious significance. Representations of the Buddha, for example, must be placed at a respectful height in the room, certainly no lower than eye-height. Even more importantly, they must be used in appropriate ways, not for example as a coffee table, a hat rack or (as in one extraordinarily thoughtless incident) as a bathroom ornament – all of which would outrage the average local. Small Buddhist pendants and carvings should also not be misused as jewellery.

1   In cases where locals are angry at foreigners for not respecting religious items in appropriate ways, who does the author support – the foreigners or the locals? _____

2   Based on what you have read, do you think it is likely that the author supports the use of religious items for decorative purposes? _____

Reading comparisons/contrasts

READ ME   The following examples include most of the basic structures for comparing. Make sure that you can recognise comparisons and understand them immediately when you see them in a reading passage.

EXAMPLE   This methodology is widely considered to be <u>much more effective than</u> the previous predominant method.

Mobile telephones are <u>much thinner than</u> they used to be.

Of the various strains of this crop, this new hybrid produces <u>by far the highest</u> yields.

This building is <u>much bigger</u> and <u>much more beautiful than</u> that building. In fact, it is <u>easily the biggest</u> and <u>most beautiful building</u> I have ever seen.

READ ME   In the following sentences the writer is comparing two situations or events. Another word for this is 'contrasting', that is, looking at and expressing the difference in two situations or events. Words that indicate structures used for contrasting are underlined in the sentences.

EXAMPLE   <u>Although</u> New Zealand was the second largest source of immigrants to Australia in the 1980s, it has yielded a declining number and proportion of settlers since 1989–90.

<u>Although</u> the number of libraries multiplied, library users remained few in number until literacy became more widespread during the 18th century.

<u>While</u> the conventional wisdom may be that all people who have reached retirement are enjoying a life of leisure, there are, in fact, a sizeable number of aged workers.

Net population gains through interstate migration have been experienced in Queensland and Western Australia. In Victoria and Tasmania, <u>on the other hand</u>, net losses have occurred.

The Olympic Games are supposed to replace the rancour of international conflict with friendly competition. In recent times, <u>however</u>, that lofty ideal has not always been attained.

The main difference between the more recent and older teaching materials is that vocabulary and grammar are no longer taught by using long quotations from literature or endless repetitions of isolated sentences. <u>Rather</u>, they are taught in the context of everyday situations.

Most countries have now established their own national libraries, <u>but</u> their oldest university libraries often have richer collections of rare materials.

READ ME   When describing a situation that is in contrast to expectations, writers frequently use the expressions 'despite' and 'in spite of'. For example, if you know that Mr Jones is rich, you might expect him to live in a big house. But, in fact, he lives in a small house. Therefore you might write:

EXAMPLE   In spite of his wealth, Mr Jones lived very simply in a one-room cottage.

OR

Mr Jones lived very simply in a one-room cottage despite his wealth.

Here is another example.

Mr Smith was found innocent in spite of having confessed to the murder.

OR

Despite having confessed to the murder Mr Smith was found innocent.

Exercise 19: Reading contrasts

Use your understanding of *in spite of* and *despite* to complete the following sentences.

1   In spite of every effort by the team of doctors, the young boy _____.

2   _____ despite the fact that she hadn't studied for it at all.

Reading examples

READ ME   It is common in both descriptive and argumentative texts to give examples. In the following sentences the writer is giving examples.

EXAMPLE   Some languages, such as Japanese, have only pitch accent, but others, like English, utilise both loudness and pitch.

People like you really deserve success.

Among the many instances of modern urban crime none is more disturbing than house invasions.

Exercise 20: Reading examples

Read the following paragraph and answer the questions below.

The emigration of highly skilled persons – the so-called 'brain drain' – has been causing concern for some years. For example, unpublished figures show that more than 5000 medical, engineering, business and other professional workers emigrated permanently in the period 1989–90.

1   What does 'brain drain' refer to?

_____

2   Give two examples of what is meant by 'highly skilled persons'?

_____

Reading reasons

READ ME As you are reading, it is important to follow the reasons that writers give to explain events or situations. Another term for reason is 'cause' and another term for the situation or event that consequently happens is 'effect'. The following examples include some of the basic structures for describing cause and effect.

EXAMPLE They selected this apartment <u>because of</u> its location.

Population aging <u>is mainly due to</u> a decline in fertility.

The 1982–83 recession <u>resulted in</u> a reduction in the total migrant intake in 1983–84.

It has been clearly demonstrated that smoking <u>leads to</u> heart disease and cancer.

You can practise reading other examples of cause and effect sentences in Exercise 21.

Exercise 21: Reading causes and effects

In the following sentences decide which comes first, the cause or the effect. If the cause comes first, write *cause/effect*. If the effect comes first, write *effect/cause*.

1 Population aging <u>is mainly due to</u> a decline in fertility.   _____*effect/cause*_____

2 We regret to announce that the concert has had to be postponed <u>due to</u> poor weather.   _____

3 Elderly women outnumber elderly men <u>because of</u> gains in female longevity.   _____

4 The government raised the tax on alcohol. <u>As a result</u>, sales declined by 2%.   _____

5 The 1982–83 recession <u>resulted in</u> a reduction in the total migrant intake in 1983–84.   _____

6 The fall in the number of people smoking <u>can be attributed to</u> education programs.   _____

7 The high number of visa over-stayers <u>is a direct consequence of</u> economic conditions.   _____

8 It has been clearly demonstrated that smoking <u>leads to</u> heart disease and cancer.   _____

9 Immigration after the Second World War <u>contributed to</u> population growth.   _____

READ ME Now you are ready to do some more practice. In Exercises 22–28 the fundamental skill needed is understanding what the writer is doing, that is, recognising the language that writers use to describe and argue. Remember that in the IELTS reading module you have limited time. To prepare for this, you should do these exercises as quickly as you can. To guide you, there is a time limit suggested for each exercise.

Exercise 22: Seeing what the writer is doing

Read the following paragraph and then circle the correct answer.   **Time limit: 1 minute**

Life forms that in some manner cause injury to human food supplies or living areas or that act as parasites or disease vectors are considered pests, and efforts to deal with these life forms are known as pest control.

What is the writer doing in this paragraph?

A defining pest control

B arguing against pest control

C describing types of pests

D comparing pests

Exercise 23: Seeing what the writer is doing

Read the paragraph and then choose the most appropriate title. Circle the correct answer.
Time limit: 1 minute

A computer virus is a computer code that is designed to change the way a computer works. Most computer viruses produce a humorous message and cause no significant damage. Others, however, are designed to inflict quite considerable disruption or damage.

A Computer viruses: How big are they?

B Computer viruses: How can you fix them?

C Computer viruses: What are they?

D Computer viruses: Who created them?

Exercise 24: Seeing what the writer is doing

Read the passage and answer the question below.   **Time limit: 5 minutes**

The Japanese tea ceremony

1   The Japanese tea ceremony, or cha-no-yu, is the ancient practice of serving tea according to a strict ritual that defines the manner in which tea is prepared and served.

2   Rooted in Zen Buddhism, the art of the tea ceremony symbolises aesthetic simplicity through the elimination of the unnecessary.

3   The ceremony as practised today takes place in a tea room, or cha-shitsu, situated in a garden or in a house. The most formal ceremony takes four hours and two types of green tea are served. Following a prescribed pattern, the host prepares the tea with the utmost exactness.

4   The tea ceremony was originated in China by Buddhist monks who believed that tea had medicinal qualities. It was brought to Japan in the 13th century, but it was not until the 16th century that Zen monks had mastered, codified and ennobled the drinking of tea.

... continued over

... continued

Which paragraph (1 to 4) contains the following information?

A A description of the tea ceremony

_____

B A definition of the tea ceremony

_____

C An account of the history of the
      tea ceremony

_____

D The significance of the tea ceremony

_____

Exercise 25: Seeing what the writer is doing

Read the passage and answer the question below.   **Time limit: 5 minutes**

Chess

1 Chess is a game for two people played on a square board of eight rows of eight squares
      each, alternately light and dark in colour.

2 The object of chess is for one player to capture the other's king. When an opposing piece
      threatens a king, the king is said to be in check. When a check cannot be averted, the
      king is said to be captured, mated or checkmated, and the game is over.

3 Certain similarities exist between the modern game of chess and an Indian game called
      chaturanga, which dates back to about the 6th century AD. The modern era of chess,
      however, may be said to date back to about the 15th century when the pieces gained
      their present form.

4 Many authorities regard the Cuban player Jose Paul Capablanca as the greatest in the
      history of chess. Bobby Fischer, an American, has been promoted by numerous experts,
      however, as Capablanca's superior.

Match the following headings with paragraphs 1 to 4.

A Chess masters

_____

B The rules of chess

_____

C Chess

_____

D The history of chess

_____

Exercise 26: Seeing what the writer is doing

Read the passage and answer the question below.   **Time limit: 7 minutes**

Internal migration in Australia

1 Permanent residential relocation within one country, or 'internal migration' as it is commonly known, is a common event in Australia. Indeed, Australians change their place of residence more frequently than people in most other countries of the world. The majority of permanent residential relocation occurs over short distances, though 12 per cent of all movers each year move interstate.

2 Interstate migration can have a large impact on the population growth and distribution of both the source State and the destination State. For example, over the 10 years 1976–86 net interstate migration (the number of people who moved to a State less the number who left) made up 35 per cent of Queensland's population growth and 15 per cent of the Northern Territory's population growth. In contrast, South Australia (18 per cent) and Victoria (22 per cent) experienced net losses from immigration.

3 In June 1986, 711 200 people were living in a different State from that in which they had been living in 1981. Net population gains through interstate migration have been experienced by Queensland, Western Australia, the Northern Territory and the Australian Capital Territory, and net losses have occurred in New South Wales, Victoria, South Australia and Tasmania. In general, the direction of net interstate migration has been northwards (on the east coast) and westwards (to the west coast).

4 The recent analysis of immigrant arrival data clearly shows that the birthplace of immigrants has a bearing on where they choose to live. For example, immigrants from Hong Kong and the Philippines, the most rapidly growing immigrant source countries, have tended to concentrate in Sydney (New South Wales), while New Zealand citizens have preferred to settle in Brisbane (Queensland).

    1 Match the following headings with paragraphs 1 to 4

       A Internal migration   _____

       B The pattern of interstate movement   _____

       C Settlement patterns of settler arrivals   _____

       D The contribution of internal migration
          to state population growth   _____

    2 What is the writer doing in paragraph 4? Circle the correct answer.

       A Drawing a conclusion and giving evidence to support this conclusion.

       B Predicting something about the future.

       C Adding extra information and then defining this information.

       D Describing a process and drawing a conclusion.

Exercise 27: Seeing what the writer is doing

Read the passage and answer the question below.   **Time limit: 3 minutes**

Heroin

1 Heroin is an opiate, meaning a drug derived from opium. More directly, heroin is made from the opium constituent morphine and is also called diacetylmorphine.

2 It was first developed in Germany in 1898 as a stronger and supposedly non-addictive form of morphine. The name was originally a trade name that anticipated heroic achievements by the drug in medical practice.

3 Heroin, morphine, and other opium derivatives are powerful narcotic analgesic drugs. They are known as 'narcotic' analgesics because they can induce sleep (or, in excessive amounts, coma). They also induce a sense of euphoria through interaction with the brain's opiate receptors.

4 Within a few years of heroin's introduction, physicians learned that it was in fact highly addictive. By 1924 the United States made its medical use illegal, followed thereafter by most other nations of the world. Heroin instead became one of the most frequently abused drugs. It is used either alone or combined with cocaine or amphetamines under such street names as 'speedballs'. The use of a synthetic opiate methadone in heroin recovery programs has aroused controversy.

Which paragraph (1 to 4) contains the following information?

A The history of the development of heroin   _____

B A description of the characteristics of heroin _____

C A definition of heroin   _____

Exercise 28: Seeing what the writer is doing

Read the passage and answer the question below.   **Time limit: 3 minutes**

Computer crime

1 Computer crime is generally defined as any crime accomplished through special knowledge of computer technology.

2 Computers have been used for most kinds of crime, including fraud, theft, larceny, embezzlement, burglary, sabotage, espionage, murder and forgery, since the first cases were reported in 1958.

3 One study of computer crimes established that most of them were committed by trusted computer users within businesses – persons with the requisite skills, knowledge, access and resources.

4 Much of known computer crime has consisted of entering false data into computers, which is simpler and safer than the complex process of writing a program to change data already in the computer.

5 There are no valid statistics about the extent of computer crime. Victims often resist reporting suspected cases because they can lose more from embarrassment, lost reputation, litigation and other consequential losses than from the acts themselves.

Which paragraphs (1 to 5) answer the following questions?

A How much computer crime is there?   _____

B What is computer crime?   _____

C Who commits computer crime?   _____

D How is computer crime carried out?   _____

E What kinds of computer crime are there?   _____

Reading diagrams

READ ME

In most subjects at university or college you must be able to read diagrams, tables and graphs. In the IELTS reading module, one passage may contain non-verbal materials such as diagrams, tables, graphs or illustrations. You must be able to read these materials quickly and effectively during the reading module. This ability is also important when you are doing the IELTS writing module. Writing Task 1 (General Training and Academic) may also contain diagrams, tables, graphs or illustrations that you must read and describe in writing.

Diagrams, tables and graphs have many similarities to reading passages. They have titles or headings and they give information. The writer is doing something in the diagram, table or graph; for example, comparing and classifying things, showing relationships or describing trends and processes. A diagram, table or graph can be written about, just as a passage can often be turned into a diagram, table or graph.

When reading a diagram, table or graph, use the same three-step strategy as for reading passages.

The three-step strategy for reading diagrams

- SKIM the diagram to get a general understanding of what the writer is doing in the diagram.

- SCAN the diagram to locate the specific information needed to answer a question.

READ this information INTENSIVELY to decide on the answer.

EXAMPLE

For example, look at how you can use this three-step approach to read the graph in Exercise 29.

1 Skim the graph quickly to get a general understanding. You can see the title 'Average Age at Marriage, 1976 and 1989'. Look at the horizontal line (called the x-axis in a graph) and you can see that this gives information about the years. Look at the vertical line (called the y-axis in a graph) and you can see that this gives information about the age at which people get married. The graph is comparing the average age when men and women got married in 1976 and 1989. The graph compares different years, so it is showing a trend.

2 Read the first question: At what age did men marry in 1976? You have to find information about men in 1976. Scan the graph and locate it on the x-axis.

3 Now look at that information closely. Check it against the y-axis, the average age at marriage. Find your answer there.

Exercise 29: Using the three-step strategy

Look at the graph and answer the following questions.

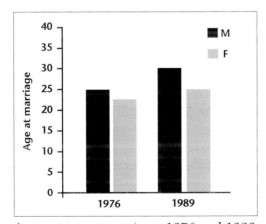

Average age at marriage, 1976 and 1989

1 At what age did men marry in 1976? _____

2 Has the average age at which women marry
risen or fallen in the period 1976–89? _____

Exercises 30 and 31 give you practice in reading tables and graphs effectively and efficiently.

Exercise 30: Reading graphs

Draw a line graph that accurately presents the information in the passage.

Income tax in the United States

Income tax was first incorporated into the constitution of the United States in 1913. This law established a progressive tax structure, which means that taxpayers are taxed at a higher percentage rate the higher their incomes are. The tax structure has remained progressive since the tax was established, although specific rates have varied greatly.

From an initial top rate of 7% in 1913, the top rate rose to 77% by 1918 to help finance World War I. The top rate fell to 25% from 1925 to 1928, but by 1936 had risen again to 78%. The highest top bracket was 94% in 1944 and 1945 to help finance World War II, and it remained above 90% in the early 1960s until it was reduced to 70% by the tax act of 1964. In 1981 the top rate was reduced to 50%, and it was reduced again by the Tax Reform Act of 1986. In 1991 the top rate was 31%.

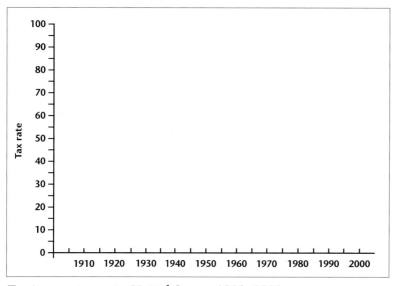

Top income tax rate, United States, 1913–1991

Exercise 31: Reading tables

Complete the table on the next page using information from the passage.

Since the late 1960s the number of children in preschool programs has greatly increased, whereas the total number of children under age five has decreased since 1960 although their numbers rose in the 1980s. The percentage of children enrolled in preschool programs rose from about 27% in 1966 to 55% in 1986. In October 1986 there were 5 971 000 children enrolled in preschool programs – 3 157 000 five-year-olds, 1 772 000 four-year-olds, and 1 041 000 three-year-olds. This represented 86.7% of the five-year-olds in the community, 49% of the four-year-olds in the community, and 28.9% of the three-year-olds in the community.

... continued over

... continued

Enrolment in preschool programs by age group, 1986

Age	3 years	4 years	5 years
Number			
% of same age group in the community			

MATCHING INFORMATION

READ ME Successful reading means being able to see the relationships between different words, that is, being able to match information. Understanding every word does not necessarily mean that you are a successful reader.

EXAMPLE Read this paragraph, for example.

> How do we humans produce speech? First the brain issues a command to the lungs to initiate an airstream. Before this airstream can become speech, however, <u>it</u> must pass through, or by, the larynx, pharynx, tongue, teeth, lips and nose – <u>all of which</u> can modify the airstream in various ways.

You might understand every word in the paragraph but you need to see the relationship of the words to one another to be a successful reader. You have to see what 'it' and 'all of which' relate to. 'It' relates to 'the airstream' and 'all of which' relates to 'the larynx, pharynx, tongue, teeth, lips and nose'.

Matching references

READ ME When reading you need to understand 'references', that is, how one word refers to other words. If you can't understand all the references, you can't understand the passage.

EXAMPLE The most typical example of a reference is a pronoun referring to a noun. Look at the following example.

> Sandra's closest friends are Amy and Lee. <u>They</u> study with <u>her</u> at the university, which is right near <u>their</u> house.

How can you find the references? When the reference word is a pronoun, look for a previous noun that might match the pronoun. Make sure that they match in gender (male or female), number (singular and plural), and case (is the word a subject, an object or a possessive?). Replace the pronoun with this noun and check to see if the meaning is possible. For example, in the sentence above, when 'her' is replaced with 'Sandra' the sentence makes sense. Therefore 'her' refers to 'Sandra'.

> Sandra
>
> Sandra's closest friends are Amy and Lee. They study with ~~her~~ at the university.

Exercise 32: Matching references

What do the underlined words refer to?

The local cafe is as much of an institution in Poland as the local pub in some English-speaking countries. Even small towns and larger villages have cafes, and in the cities there are hundreds of (1) them. They are always well patronised, the reason being that local cafes are ideal spots for meeting friends and for stopping at during long walks. (2) They also have the right atmosphere to entertain friends, the privacy to discuss business and the convenience simply to gossip for a while over a glass of wine or an espresso coffee and a piece of cake. For retired people, spending a few hours at a cafe over a cup of coffee watching other people is probably better entertainment than watching television. When Poles go out to spend some time with friends, especially when (3) they date or meet informally, they prefer to go to a cafe than to a restaurant. They either stay (4) there for the whole evening or proceed to other places.

Most young people in Poland enjoy similar forms of entertainment as (5) their peers in English-speaking countries. (6) These include popular music concerts, discos, movies, sporting events – soccer being by far the most popular sport in Poland – and attractions available in the city or local centre. People with children, as elsewhere, tend to go out less, especially if (7) they do not have parents or in-laws to look after the children. (8) They tend to go for walks in local parks or visit other people with children.

1 _____   5 _____

2 _____   6 _____

3 _____   7 _____

4 _____   8 _____

Exercise 33: Matching references

What do the underlined words refer to?

The flows of illegal immigrants have persisted in a number of countries. (1) These flows have been fostered by the demographic imbalance between the developed and the developing countries, differentials in economic growth, employment opportunities and wages, and a demand for low-wage workers in a number of developed countries.

Although some countries have sought to strengthen the sovereignty of (2) their frontiers through such measures as the extension of visa requirements and increased checks on employers to ensure (3) they have not hired illegals, illegal immigration still continues.

For example, the scale of illegal immigration to the United States is massive. It has been estimated that three million illegals enter the United States successfully every year with perhaps twenty five per cent of (4) them remaining permanently.

1 _____   3 _____

2 _____   4 _____

Matching statements

READ ME One common type of task requires you to decide whether a statement is 'true', 'false' or 'not given' according to the passage. In deciding this, you are matching two statements: the statement given in the question and the statement given in the passage.

EXAMPLE Here are two examples.

> • One of the statements given in the question is:
>
>   *Over five million illegals enter each year. True, False or Not given?*
>
>   When you scan the passage, you locate this statement:
>
>   *Three million illegals enter every year.*
>
>   The two statements do not match so the answer is 'false'.
>
> • Another question about the passage is:
>
>   *Most migrants marry other migrants. True, False or Not given?*
>
>   When you scan the passage, you cannot locate any statements about this. The answer is therefore 'not given'.

READ ME In answering *True/False/Not given* tasks, there are three questions to ask yourself:

- Do the words that specify the nouns match?
- Do the words that specify verbs match?
- Do the facts match?

These three questions are examined below.

Words that specify nouns

READ ME In *True/False/Not given* questions, you are asked to compare two pieces of information: the statement given in the test question and the statement given in the passage. Sometimes the difference between the two is in the words that specify the nouns.

A noun is a word that gives the name of something, for example, 'book', 'father', 'knowledge' and 'university'. When people want to talk about something, they must specify, that is, they must say which noun they are talking about. Look at the different ways of specifying the noun 'book'. Note that specifying words can become before or after the noun.

- <u>all</u> books
- <u>this</u> book
- <u>the</u> book <u>that I found</u>
- <u>that</u> red book
- <u>that</u> book <u>about grammar</u>

In *True/False/Not given* questions, you must check whether the nouns are the same in the statement and in the passage. Are they specified in the same way?

Some examples are given below. In all of these examples the correct answer in an IELTS test would be 'false'. The information does not match. The specific meanings are not the same.

EXAMPLE

What you read in the question	What you read in the passage	Answer
people <u>who have heart disease</u>	<u>all</u> people	F
<u>some</u> of the problems	<u>most</u> of the problems	F
<u>difficult</u> questions	<u>important</u> questions	F
people <u>at work</u>	people <u>at home</u>	F

READ ME   In grammatical terms, these different ways of specifying nouns are called:

- relative clauses, eg *who have heart disease*
- quantifiers, eg *most, all, some*
- demonstrative pronouns, eg *this*
- prepositional phrases, eg *at home*
- adjectives, eg *difficult*

Exercise 34: Words that specify nouns

Answer the following questions.

1   Look at the pen in your hand. Which pen are you looking at? Be specific.

   A   I'm looking at _____. (answer with a demonstrative pronoun)

   B   I'm looking at _____. (answer with a prepositional phrase)

   C   I'm looking at _____. (answer with an adjective)

2   Which people do you like? Be specific.

   A   I like _____. (answer with a quantifier)

   B   I like _____. (answer with a relative clause)

   C   I like _____. (answer with an adjective)

3   Which tests do you hate? Be specific.

   A   I hate _____. (answer with a quantifier)

   B   I hate _____. (answer with a relative clause)

   C   I hate _____. (answer with an adjective)

Exercise 35: Answering *True/False/Not given* questions

Are the statements below *True, False* or *Not given* according to the paragraph? Circle T, F or NG.

The banana comes in all kinds of sizes and shapes. Its plant, which may reach eight metres in height, bears big hanging purple flowers, and almost every part of it is useable.

1	You can use every part of a banana.	T	F	NG
2	Some banana trees grow over eight metres high.	T	F	NG
3	The flowers on a banana tree are big and purple.	T	F	NG
4	Bananas are really delicious.	T	F	NG
5	Bananas have a standard size and shape.	T	F	NG

Words that specify verbs

READ ME Sometimes the difference between the statement given in the test question and the statement given in the passage is in the words that specify the verbs.

EXAMPLE We use verbs to describe what nouns do and to say what condition or situation these nouns are in. For example:

- <u>eat</u> bananas

- <u>write</u> books

- the bananas <u>look</u> delicious

- the books <u>are lying</u> on the floor

As we saw with nouns, when writers want to talk about something, they often specify particular details. The table below shows the different ways of specifying the verb 'eat'. Note that specifying words can become before or after the verb.

EXAMPLE

Specifying verbs	Examples
Positive or negative Where, when, how often etc	I eat/<u>don't</u> eat bananas. I eat bananas <u>in the morning/every day</u>. I eat bananas <u>when I do my homework</u>. I <u>often</u> eat bananas.
Attitude or opinion	I <u>should/must/ought to</u> eat bananas.

Look at the examples below. In all of these examples the correct answers in an IELTS test would be 'false'. The information specifying the verbs does not match.

EXAMPLE

What you read in the question	What you read in the passage	Answer
He <u>can</u> travel. Women <u>always</u> drive carefully. He sews <u>while he watches TV</u>.	He <u>should</u> travel. Women <u>usually</u> drive carefully. He sews <u>in the evening</u>.	F F F

In grammatical terms, these different ways of specifying verbs are called:

- modal auxiliary verbs, eg *can, should, must, ought to*
- adverbs, eg *always, usually, often, carefully*
- adverbial phrases, eg *in the evening, on the floor*
- adverbial clauses, eg *while he watches TV, when I do my homework*

Exercise 36: Words which specify verbs

1 Where do you do your homework? Be specific.

I do my homework _____. (answer with an adverbial phrase)

2 When do you do your homework? Be specific.

I do my homework _____. (answer with an adverbial phrase)

3 Do you like doing homework? Be specific.

I _____ homework. (answer positive or negative)

4 What do you do while you are doing your homework? Be specific.

I _____. (answer with an adverbial clause)

Exercise 37: Answering *True/False/Not given* questions

Are the statements below *True*, *False* or *Not given* according to the paragraph? Circle T, F or NG.

Widely popular in Asia, the guava is little known in Western countries, although it is both delicious and nutritious, with a very high Vitamin C content. Its pear-like crunchy flesh is best eaten unripe.

1 The guava is widely popular in Asia.	T	F	NG
2 Guavas must be eaten unripe.	T	F	NG
3 Guavas are unknown in Western countries.	T	F	NG
4 Guavas are usually eaten for breakfast.	T	F	NG
5 Guavas are often eaten with a bit of salt.	T	F	NG

The accuracy of facts

READ ME Sometimes the difference between the statement given in the test question and the statement given in the reading passage is in the accuracy of the information provided. This applies both to words that specify nouns and to words that specify verbs.

When the answer is false

READ ME In all the following examples the correct answer in an IELTS test would be 'false'. The information does not match.

What you read in the question	What you read in the passage	Answer
I answered <u>fifteen</u> questions.	I answered <u>fourteen</u> questions.	F
We used to <u>stay in</u> a flat.	We used to <u>own</u> a flat.	F
He arrived in <u>November</u>.	He arrived in <u>December</u>.	F

When the answer is true

READ ME   Note that the two statements might use different words but have the same meaning and therefore the correct answer would be 'true'. The answer to each example below is 'true'.

EXAMPLE

What you read in the question	What you read in the passage	Answer
He should go to a doctor.	He ought to see a doctor.	T
Mary's children really like sports.	Mary said, 'My kids are keen on sport'.	T

In the first example, 'should' and 'ought to' are very similar in meaning, as are 'go to a doctor' and 'see a doctor'. In the second example, 'children' and 'kids' are the same, as are 'really like' and 'be keen on'.

When the answer is not given

READ ME   In *True/False/Not given* questions, a 'not given' answer means that it is not possible to determine whether the statement is true or false – the passage does not give enough relevant information to make this choice.

In the following examples, the answer in all cases is 'not given'.

EXAMPLE

What you read in the question	What you read in the passage	Answer
They produce the best cars.	Their cars are expensive.	NG
Computers have many uses.	Computers are popular.	NG
Bananas are nutritious.	Bananas taste really good.	NG

Now look at the sample exercise on the next page. Remember that you are asked whether the statements are *True*, *False* or *Not given* according to the passage. It doesn't matter whether you personally agree with the passage.

EXAMPLE

> Are the statements below *True*, *False* or *Not given* according to the paragraph? Circle T, F or NG.
>
> Research indicates that, if adults and children are given the same amount of time to learn a foreign language, it is the adults who will be more successful, with the possible exception of achieving a native-like pronunciation.
>
> | | | | | |
> |---|---|---|---|---|
> | **1** | Adults enjoy learning foreign languages more than children do. | T | F | NG |
> | **2** | Foreign languages are difficult to learn. | T | F | NG |
> | **3** | There has been extensive research into the learning of foreign languages. | T | F | NG |

For all three statements, the correct answer would be 'not given'. In statement 1, you do not know if they 'enjoy' the learning. You only know which one is more 'successful'. Maybe they enjoy it more, maybe they don't. This information is 'not given'. In statement 2, you do not know if foreign languages are difficult to learn (remember: your personal opinion does not count!). You only know that research says adults are more successful than children. Maybe foreign languages are difficult; maybe they aren't. This information is 'not given'. In statement 3, you do not know how much research there has been. You only know about one type of research.

Exercise 38: Answering *True/False/Not given* questions

Are the statements below *True*, *False* or *Not given* according to the passage? Circle T, F or NG.

The Olympic Games are an international sports festival that began in ancient Greece. The original Greek games were staged every fourth year for several hundred years until they were abolished in the early Christian era.

The revival of the Olympic Games took place in 1896 and since then they have been staged every four years, except during World War I and World War II (1916, 1940, 1944).

Perhaps the basic difference between the ancient and modern Olympics is that the former were the ancient Greeks' way of saluting their gods, whereas the modern Games are a manner of saluting the athletic talents of citizens of all nations. The original Olympics featured competition in music, oratory and theatre performances as well. The modern Games have a more expansive athletic agenda, and for two and a half weeks they are supposed to replace the rancour of international conflict with friendly competition. In recent times, however, that lofty ideal has not always been attained.

1	The ancient Olympics lasted for several hundred years.	T	F	NG
2	The modern Olympics have been held every four years since 1896.	T	F	NG
3	The ancient and modern Olympics have the same basic aim.	T	F	NG
4	The modern Olympics have more kinds of athletics.	T	F	NG
5	The ideal of the modern Games has not been achieved.	T	F	NG

Exercise 39: Answering *True/False/Not given* questions

Are the statements below *True*, *False* or *Not given* according to the paragraph? Circle T, F or NG.

Research indicates that if adults and children are given the same amount of time to learn a foreign language, it is the adults who will be more successful, with the possible exception of achieving a native-like pronunciation.

1	Adults find it easy to learn foreign languages.	T	F	NG
2	The issue of whether adults or children learn foreign languages more successfully has been researched.	T	F	NG
3	It has been concluded that children are more successful than adults at achieving a native-like pronunciation in a foreign language.	T	F	NG

Exercise 40: Answering *True/False/Not given* questions

Are the statements below *True*, *False* or *Not given* according to the paragraph? Circle T, F or NG.

Despite the dazzling diversity of shape and colour among insects, they all share three fundamental characteristics in common. They are made up of three component parts. All are invertebrates, that is, they have no backbone. And, finally, all have six legs.

1	Insects are often very different in their shape and colour.	T	F	NG
2	All insects share the same shape and colour.	T	F	NG
3	Insects are a vital part of the environment.	T	F	NG
4	Insects have no backbone.	T	F	NG
5	Insects share many of the same characteristics as other animals.	T	F	NG

5 Developing your study program

To prepare for the IELTS reading module you need to devise a study program that will help you develop your reading strategies and skills.

- First decide what your needs are.
- Then choose some passages to read for practice.
- Then practise the strategies and skills required by the reading module.

DECIDING YOUR NEEDS

Think about what you need. Do you need, for example, to focus on expanding your vocabulary? Do you need to practise matching references? Do you need to check your understanding of what is in the reading module? Complete the following checklist to help you to think about your needs.

Reading checklist	(✔)
Do you know what is in the reading module?	( )
Do you know:	
how long the reading module lasts?	( )
how long the reading passages are?	( )
how many questions there are?	( )
the formats of the questions?	( )
Do you know what skills you need to improve your reading?	( )
Do you need to improve:	
your vocabulary?	( )
your skimming skills?	( )
your scanning skills?	( )
seeing what the writer is doing?	( )
matching 'references' accurately and quickly?	( )
matching information and deciding if statements are true, false or not given?	( )
guessing the meaning of unknown words?	( )
Do you have a study plan to develop your reading skills?	( )
Do you read English every day?	( )
Are you learning new vocabulary every day?	( )
Can you state ten new words that you have learned in the past week?	( )
Do you try different exercises when you read?	( )

FINDING APPROPRIATE PASSAGES TO PRACTISE READING

READ ME

Choosing texts that you find interesting is important. If your reading is enjoyable, you will probably read more often and that's good for your reading skills!

Like any other skill, the ability to read a foreign language requires a lot of regular practice, especially if your goal is to be able to read accurately and quickly. As a general guideline, you should do at least 30 minutes of focused reading every day. As your study program progresses, you should practise more specific exercises as suggested below. Remember that it takes a long time to become as efficient a reader in a foreign language as you are in your own.

Look for reading passages in the following:

- Textbooks used in either high school or university. The textbooks can be on any subject, for example, history, geography, accounting or social science. Textbooks that contain some diagrams, tables and graphs are particularly useful.

- Textbooks that teach English, either at an intermediate or advanced level. Focus particularly on reading passages, but sections on grammar and vocabulary and writing skills can also be useful.

- English-language newspapers, either foreign or local. Read articles that you find interesting, whether sport, politics, current events or even the comic strips. Use a mix of skimming and reading intensively.

- Popular magazines such as *Time*, *Newsweek* and *Reader's Digest*. Choose articles that you find interesting.

- Encyclopedias. Skim through the list of contents or index and select those entries that you find interesting.

- Novels. Choose any type of short story or novel that you think you will enjoy.

You may feel that some of these suggestions are not academic enough but they can be useful in your IELTS test preparation. With any of these texts, you can:

- expand your vocabulary by selecting and learning useful words in the way you practised in Exercises 7 and 8, for example; and

- practise all of the reading skills presented in this unit, for example: deciding what the writer is doing (such as in Exercise 22), matching references (such as in Exercise 32), and guessing the meaning of unknown words (such as in Exercises 9 and 10).

PRACTISING THE SKILLS NEEDED FOR THE READING MODULE

Exercises for independent study

Here are some exercises you can do by yourself. You can do them before you read a passage, while you read it and after you read it.

Before reading a passage, anticipate

Anticipate as much as you can about what you are going to read.

For example, you are going to read a passage entitled 'Modern methods of language teaching'. What do you think the writer is going to talk about? It is reasonable to anticipate that the article may contain descriptions of methods, a description of how the methods were developed, and an evaluation of the strengths and weaknesses of various methods. After anticipating the content, read the article and see how accurate your predictions were.

Anticipate questions

After you have read a passage, think of the questions that might be asked about it. For example, if you read a passage about budget travel you might anticipate questions like: What types are budget travel are there? Which method of travel is the cheapest? Which destinations are the most popular? What are the advantages of budget travel? What are the problems associated with budget travel?

Underline pronouns and decide what they refer to

Select a short reading passage and underline every pronoun you can see. Then decide what these pronouns refer to.

Look at Exercise 32 as an example.

Ask yourself what the writer is doing

As you read, ask yourself what the writer is doing (such as defining, giving examples, describing cause and effect). Decide what headings you would give to each paragraph.

Look at Exercises 22 to 28 as examples.

Guess the meanings of words

Select a short reading passage and underline every word you don't know. Guess the meaning of the words and then check your guesses in a dictionary.

Look at Exercises 9 and 10 as examples.

Write a short summary

When you finish reading a passage, write a short summary. This is a good way of checking how much you understand when you read. It helps you to focus on the main points.

Look at Exercise 1 as an example.

Predict what comes next

When reading a passage, occasionally stop and predict what might come next. For example, read the following paragraph. What is the writer is going to write about next?

The largest city in Thailand is the capital Bangkok. Meaning 'the village with the kok tree', Bangkok was the name of a small village that existed at the site before King Rama I moved the capital there. When this new capital was established, it was given a name of truly royal proportions and is listed as the longest place name in the world. To this day Thais call their capital by the first part of this name, Krung Thep. The vast majority of people are, however, aware that foreigners call the city Bangkok, although they themselves do not use this name.

The second largest ...

Now read the paragraph below and again, ask yourself what the writer is going to write about next.

Diamond, one of the world's most important mineral resources, is pure, natural carbon with the atoms organised in a close-packed cubic arrangement that gives the stones their hardness. Because diamond is so much harder than any other natural or artificial substance known, it is ideal for ...

In some cases, your predictions may only be broadly correct – or indeed they may be quite wrong. This does not matter: you are still developing the right skill. In other cases, you can predict very accurately what the writer's next words will be. To do this, however, you need to know a considerable range of vocabulary. The more you expand your vocabulary (by listening and reading), the easier it is to make accurate predictions.

READ ME

Exercises with study partners

Here are some exercises you can do with a partner.

Tell your partner what you have read

Read a short passage once only, writing a few notes as you read. Using these notes and without looking at the passage, tell your partner what you have read.

Write *True/False/Not given* questions

Choose a reading passage. Write a series of statements based on information in the passage. Make some of the statements true, some of them false and include some statements for which there is no relevant information given. Give the passage and the statements to your partner.

Look at Exercise 35 as an example.

Write short-answer questions

Choose a reading passage, a diagram, table or graph. Write a series of questions based on the information in the passage or diagram. Give the passage or diagram and the statements to your partner to do within an agreed time limit.

Look at Exercise 4 as an example.

Make a gap-filling exercise

Ask your partner to choose a short passage, make a photocopy and delete every sixth word (or every tenth word or, to make the exercise more difficult, every third word). Your task is to guess the missing words. Check the original passage to see how accurate you were.

Guess the missing words

READ ME Ask your partner to select a short passage. Your partner then numbers each of the words in the passage and retains this copy, and makes a second copy, again numbering each of the words. This time your partner deletes the letters and replaces them with dashes. Your partner gives you this copy. Your task is to guess the missing words. For example, if you guess 'is', your partner will tell you each of the numbers where the word appears. In the example below 'is' appears at 4 and 20. Fill them in on your copy and then take another guess, continuing until you complete all the gaps.

EXAMPLE Here is an example of a paragraph that your partner might select.

Papua New Guinea is an island nation located at the western end of the Pacific Ocean. The main island is crossed by mountain ranges including a number of peaks over 4000 metres high.

And here is the copy of the paragraph your partner gives to you.

Papua New Guinea 4_____ 5_____ 6_____ 7_____ 8_____ 9_____ 10_____ 11_____

12_____ 13_____ 14_____ 15_____ 16_____ . 17_____ 18_____ 19_____ 20_____

21_____ 22_____ 23_____ 24_____ 25_____ 26_____ 27_____ 28_____ 29_____

30_____ 31_____ 32_____ 33_____ .

6 IELTS practice tests: Reading

IELTS PRACTICE TEST: READING (GENERAL TRAINING)

All answers must be written on the Answer Sheet at the end of the test.

The test is divided as follows:

Reading Passage 1	Questions 1 to 13
Reading Passage 2	Questions 14 to 25
Reading Passage 3	Questions 26 to 40

Start at the beginning of the test and work through it. You should answer all the questions. If you cannot do a particular question leave it and go on to the next one. You can return to it later.

TIME ALLOWED: 60 MINUTES

READING PASSAGE 1

You should spend about 20 minutes on Questions 1 to 13.

Questions 1 to 13

Look at the list of eight television series (**A–H**). Answer the questions below by writing the letters of the appropriate series **A–H** in boxes 1 to 13 on your answer sheet.

NB   You may use any letter more than once.

Example   **Answer**

Which series looks at Chinese history?   **B**

1   Which series has won awards?

2   Which TWO series are screened on Friday?

3   Which series is NOT screened in the morning?

4   Which series shows the way people used to live?

5   Which TWO series are presented by students?

6   Which series has the most parts?

7   Which TWO series have 60-minute programs?

8   Which series would help students looking for a job?

9   Which TWO series focus on the future?

10   Which series is NOT about people?

11   Which series stresses that its topic is not as
difficult as viewers might consider?

12   Which TWO series focus on just one particular country?

13   Which series gives the meaning of words?

Education programs on Channel 7

A *A world of music:* This award-winning six-part series introduces music from an international perspective. Featuring musicians from five continents, each 30-minute program focuses on the origin of music and the role of music in people's lives. Tuesday 7.30am and Friday 7.00am.

B *Ancient civilisations:* How do civilisations begin? Why do they fall? This five-part series looks for answers to these questions in the ancient civilisations of Rome, meso-America and China. Each 30-minute program includes computer-generated reconstructions of daily life in these societies. Saturday 5.00am.

C *Mathematics and you:* This innovative 12-part series takes the sting out of mathematics. Presented by secondary students, each 15-minute program shows how mathematics relates to your daily life. Explanations and examples are easy to follow and fun. Tuesday 6.00am.

D *Working life:* This series looks at jobs in various employment sectors such as the hospitality industry, information technology, horticulture and childcare. Each of the 20-minute programs in the ten-part series follows a person who actually works in that sector. Friday 5.00am.

E *The last millennium?* As we enter the third millennium, the question arises: will this be the last? Will the world succumb to environmental degradation? Using a case-study approach, each 60-minute program in this three-part series takes a detailed look at an environmental problem. How will this problem affect the people living in that area? What are the implications globally? Saturday 7.00am.

F *Faces in the news:* This ten-part series examines two people who have been in the news limelight during the last year. Each ten-minute program presents the original news reports, provides background information, summarises the main points of the report and explains the vocabulary used in the reports. Monday 7.00am.

G *Naturally England:* This four-part series examines the natural environment in England. Each 60-minute program explores a different season, outlining the interaction of climate, plants and animals. Both informative and beautiful, the series has been nominated for two cinematography awards. Tuesday 5.00am.

H *The USA and IT:* This three-part series takes a look at information technology in the United States of America in the coming twenty-first century. In this new so-called 'information age' how will people study, work, communicate and identify themselves? Each 30-minute program is presented by students. Wednesday 11.00pm.

READING PASSAGE 2

You should spend about 20 minutes on Questions 14 to 25.

Questions 14 to 19

For each question choose the letter (**A–D**) that most closely describes the authors' claims and write the appropriate letter in boxes 14 to 19 on your answer sheet.

14 Being a good student …

   A involves many different factors.

   B is extremely important.

   C can be achieved easily.

   D may not be enjoyable.

15 A good weight for a person who is 155 cm tall is …

   A 50 kg.

   B 117 kg.

   C 65 kg.

   D 55 kg.

16 Students should eat …

   A more carbohydrates.

   B more sugar.

   C less protein.

   D more food.

17 The average student …

   A should sleep less.

   B gets enough sleep.

   C should sleep more.

   D sleeps 8 hours a day.

18 The biggest proportional shortfall in the average student's time management is in the time spent in …

   A sleeping.

   B self-study.

   C exercise and sport.

   D daily tasks and travel.

19 The centre's services are available free to …

   A people who go to see the centre.

   B students with a currently valid student card.

   C people who manage their time well.

   D people who come to the ground floor of the Haydon Building.

A ARE YOU A GOOD STUDENT OR AN AVERAGE STUDENT?

B What is a 'good' student? We think a good student is not just someone who gets good results in their study. We believe that a good student is a person who is physically healthy (in good condition and eating nutritious food) and mentally healthy (with sound self-esteem and good stress management). We think a good student can manage their time well and can enjoy – yes, enjoy – their study. Unfortunately, research shows that the average student does not achieve these goals. Are you a good student or an average student? Check out the stats and make up your own mind.

C Good student

A person whose height/weight ratio is ideal (that is, with a gap of 100 between height in centimetres and weight in kilograms). For example, a person who is 175 cm tall and weighs 75 kg.

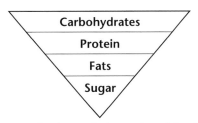

A person who has a balanced and healthy diet

A person who manages their time appropriately

Average student

A person whose height/weight ratio is not ideal (that is, with a gap of more than 100 between height in centimetres and weight in kilograms). For example, a person who is 175 cm tall but who weighs 85 kg.

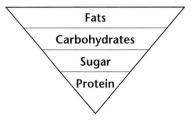

A person who does not have a balanced diet

A person who has difficulty managing their time appropriately

D STUDENT HEALTH AND SUPPORT SERVICES CENTRE

E Ground Floor, Haydon Building; Open 8am to 6pm Monday to Friday

F At the Student Health and Support Services, our staff can help you with health matters, study-related issues and personal concerns. We have doctors (both male and female), psychologists and professionally trained guidance counsellors. If we can't help you ourselves, we'll find someone who can! All our services are 100% free to students with a currently valid student card. All our services are 100% confidential.

G DON'T FORGET TO BRING YOUR STUDENT CARD WHEN YOU COME TO SEE US

Questions 20 to 25

Reading Passage 2 has seven parts labelled **A–G**.

From the list of headings below choose the most suitable heading for parts **A–G**.

Write the appropriate number (**i–x**) in boxes 20 to 25 on your answer sheet.

NB   There are more headings than parts so you will not use all of them. You may use any of the headings more than once.

List of headings
(i) The title of the passage
(ii) A reminder to students wishing to use the centre's services
(iii) The writer's philosophy
(iv) A description of the centre's organisation
(v) Information about the centre's services and staff
(vi) Information about the centre's methods
(vii) Advice about improving diets
(viii) Details about the centre's location and operating hours
(ix) The name of the centre
(x) Profiles of students' characteristics

Example	**Answer**
Part A	**(i)**

20 Part B

21 Part C

22 Part D

23 Part E

24 Part F

25 Part G

READING PASSAGE 3

You should spend about 20 minutes on Questions 26 to 40.

The United Nations

The United Nations (UN) is a general international organisation established at the end of World War II to promote international peace and security. It is the second such organisation, having replaced the League of Nations, which was founded in the aftermath of World War I.

The United Nations officially came into existence on 24 October 1945, when 51 original members ratified its charter. The main purposes of the organisation were 'to save succeeding generations from the scourge of war'; develop friendly relations among states; cooperate in solving international economic, social, cultural and humanitarian problems; and promote respect for human rights and fundamental freedoms.

To enable it to work towards its goals, the UN was equipped with six major organs: the Security Council, General Assembly, Economic and Social Council, Trusteeship Council, International Court of Justice and the Secretariat. In addition, a number of specialised agencies were attached to the UN system to deal with specific international problems.

The primary responsibility for the maintenance of international peace and security was assigned to the Security Council. Based on the assumption that the five major military contributors to victory in World War II – the United States, the USSR, Great Britain, France and China – could reach unanimity on the question of peace in the postwar world, the Security Council made up of these five members was to be the international guardian of peace.

The second major UN organ, the General Assembly, was to operate as a forum for debating world issues. The underlying assumption in creating the General Assembly was that the airing of disputes among nations could contribute to the pacific settlement of those disputes as well as to peaceful changes in the international system.

A third principal organ, the Economic and Social Council, was created in the belief that a great deal of international strife was rooted in poverty and misery and that therefore the UN should do its utmost to help raise standards of living and economic conditions throughout the world. Because, moreover, the founders of the UN saw colonialism as another frequent source of war, they felt it necessary also to employ the new world organisation to mitigate the anger of dependent peoples against their colonial masters. To devise a technique whereby independence could be gained with as little bloodshed as possible, they provided a fourth major organ, the Trusteeship Council.

Yet another cause of war was believed by the founders of the UN to lie in the absence of common legal standards among nations. For this reason they included within the UN framework a world court, the International Court of Justice.

Finally, the founders of the UN were convinced that the maintenance of peace required a nucleus of men and women whose loyalty was first and foremost not to any particular nation but to the entire international community. To form such an international civil service, they established a sixth major organ of the UN, the Secretariat headed by the secretary-general.

Questions 26 to 30

Look at the list of aims **A–J**. Choose the most suitable aim for each of the UN organs listed below. Write the appropriate letters **A–J** in boxes 26 to 30 on your answer sheet.

NB   There are more aims than UN organs so you will not use all of them. You may use any of the aims more than once.

List of aims
A   To improve living standards and economic conditions
B   To maintain international peace
C   To establish a framework
D   To establish common legal standards
E   To provide neutral administration of the UN
F   To facilitate the independence of colonised nations
G   To allow international debate
H   To set up six major organs
I   To establish a number of specialised agencies
J   To encourage loyalty to particular nations

Example   **Answer**

Security Council   **B**

26   Economic and Social Council

27   International Court of Justice

28   General Assembly

29   Trusteeship Council

30   Secretariat

Questions 31 to 40

Do the following statements reflect the statements made by the writer of Reading Passage 3?

In boxes 31 to 40 on your answer sheet write:

YES	if the statement agrees with the writer
NO	if the statement contradicts the writer
NOT GIVEN	if there is no information about this in the passage

Example   **Answer**

The League of Nations did not succeed.   **NOT GIVEN**

31   The United Nations is the first general international organisation ever established.

32   The United Nations replaced the previous League of Nations.

33   One of the reasons for setting up the UN was to avoid further war.

34   The UN established specialised agencies to handle specific international problems.

35   The five members of the Security Council became members because of their size.

36   Since the war the Security Council has been able to achieve unanimity on peace

37   The founders of the UN felt that debating in the General Assembly could help solve disputes.

38   The founders of the UN saw a connection between conflict and economic conditions.

39   The establishment of the International Court of Justice has brought common legal standards.

40   The UN has a comprehensive structure for dealing with the world's problems.

After you have completed this practice test check the Answer Key.

IELTS practice test: Reading (Academic)

All answers must be written on the Answer Sheet at the end of the test.

The test is divided as follows:

Reading Passage 1	Questions 1 to 13
Reading Passage 2	Questions 14 to 26
Reading Passage 3	Questions 27 to 40

Start at the beginning of the test and work through it. You should answer all the questions. If you cannot do a particular question leave it and go on to the next one. You can return to it later.

TIME ALLOWED: 60 MINUTES

READING PASSAGE 1

You should spend about 20 minutes on Questions 1 to 13.

Questions 1 to 7

Reading Passage 1 has 6 sections **A–H**.

From the list of headings below choose the most suitable heading for sections **A–F**.

Write the appropriate number (**i–x**) in boxes 1 to 7 on your answer sheet.

NB   There are more headings than sections so you will not use all of them. You may use any of the headings more than once.

List of headings	
(i)	The feeding habits of feral cats
(ii)	A pointless campaign
(iii)	Cats: a dangerous pet
(iv)	A more realistic campaign
(v)	An increase in the garden bird population
(vi)	A false belief
(vii)	Ways of controlling feral cats
(viii)	Garden birds: a threatened species
(ix)	Natural predators of birds
(x)	The impossibility of controlling feral cats

Example   **Answer**

Section D   **(v)**

1 Section A

2 Section B

3 Section C

4 Section E

5 Section F

6 Section G

7 Section H

Cats – scoundrels or scapegoats?

A The campaign against cats has become so exaggerated it has lost its focus. Much energy that could be put to good use is being wasted on futile campaigns that do little more than aggravate cat owners.

B It is widely believed that because cats prey on native birds they could bring about their extermination. But predation seldom leads to extinction in such a simplistic way. If it did there would be no animals left in Africa, as those big cats called Lions would have eaten them all up.

C Enormous numbers of birds are killed by pet cats in gardens, it is true. But while this may sound alarming, ecologically there is nothing wrong with it – predation is a fact of life. Birds are killed in forests too, by a whole gamut of predators including snakes, goannas, falcons, butcherbirds, quolls, dingoes and even spiders. Pet cats are the urban counterparts to a range of native predators.

D Hunting by pet cats would only be a problem if the rate of predation, combined with other deaths, exceeded the breeding rate of the birds. This does not seem to be the case. Several studies show that urban environments actually support a higher density of birds than native forests, despite all the cats. This is partly because of all the garden plants with berries and nectar rich flowers.

E The native garden birds killed by cats are nearly all widespread adaptable species that are thriving in response to urbanisation. Some of them are probably more abundant now than they were before European settlement. This definitely seems to be the case for the common garden skinks that cats often kill.

F Feral cats are a much greater threat to wildlife than pet cats, and in some situations they are a major hazard. But not usually to birds, which they seldom eat. Studies of their diet confirm what cartoonists have always known: that cats prefer rats, mice and other small mammals. In a major article on cats (*Nature Australia*, Winter 1993) Chris Dickman stated: 'In most Australian studies, rabbits constitute the single most important prey'.

G I would suggest that foxes pose a greater problem, yet there is no passionate public campaign to oust foxes, presumably because it is obvious we can never eliminate the millions of wild foxes in Australia. Yet the same common sense thinking is not applied to cats. It is thought instead that, if everyone would only spay their cats, string bells around their necks and keep them in at night, cats would no longer kill wildlife. But what of the millions of feral cats in our deserts and woodlands? They are the bigger problem, but they are no more controllable than foxes or cane toads.

H To be useful, the anti-cat campaign should focus on specific situations where cats are a proven problem, and where something can actually be done about it. But to make the sweeping claim that 'Cats threaten the future survival of most wildlife', as the Victorian Department of Environment does in a leaflet, is to exaggerate the case so badly that it probably does more harm than good, by pitting cat owners against conservationists, instead of bringing them together as allies.

Tim Low, *Nature Australia*, Autumn 1996, p 80

Questions 8 to 13

Do the following statements reflect the claims of the writer of Reading Passage 1?

In boxes 8 to 13 on your answer sheet write:

YES	if the statement agrees with the writer
NO	if the statement contradicts the writer
NOT GIVEN	if there is no information about this in the passage

8   The activity of predators, such as lions, causes extinction of other animals.

9   Other animals eat more birds than cats.

10   There are more birds per kilometre in towns and cities than in a forest environment.

11   The large number of plants in gardens has helped to increase the bird population.

12   The author believes that all wild foxes should be killed.

13   Cats are a particular problem in Victoria.

READING PASSAGE 2

You should spend about 20 minutes on questions 14 to 26.

Does an aging society mean an aging culture?

Especially in the United States, the developed world's obsession with newness, progress and the future has always derived its energy from the numerical heft of each new rising generation. As recently as 1970, when a new youth culture redefined the American dream, the US median age was only 28 – not much higher than the median (about age 18 to 20) of the typical pre-modern society. Today with the US median age hitting an unprecedented 35, the American public hears a lot less about the ideals of youth than about the worries of the middle-aged and old.

And this is just the beginning: by the year 2030, the median age will reach at least 40 in the United States and at least the late 40s in much of Europe. Back when America's baby boomers were warning each other, 'Don't trust anyone over 30', Americans over 30 were in the minority. Over the foreseeable future, they are certain to remain in a solid majority. By the year 2030, over one-half of all adults will be aged 50 and over – and thus eligible to join AARP (the American association of retired persons). While this 50 and over crowd will outnumber all younger adults in the United States, in some European countries it will outnumber all younger adults and all children.

What do these numbers mean for our culture? Clearly, they mean a much greater focus on the interests and activities of the old over those of the young. For decades, the mass media in the United States and around the world – TV, movies, popular music, and radio – have aggressively courted the all important under 50 demographic. How will the business, as well as the substance, of popular culture change as it becomes evident that the elderly represent the fastest growing component of the total population and youth the fastest shrinking one?

We should not be surprised to see pension issues eclipsing college issues on the front pages of newspapers. Yet the numbers may have a deeper influence. Along with experience and wisdom, it has long been observed that old age brings with it an aversion to risk and change. Cicero put it this way: 'young men for action, old men for counsel'. As people age, moreover, the formative era that shaped their education and outlook becomes ever more remote in time – making them seem, in a changing world, increasingly 'out of date' from the perspective of youth.

As the entire population of the developed world grows older, the attributes of personal aging may come to define the tone and pace of the culture at large.

Part of this tone may be a general slowing down of the pace of social life. As social scientist Andrew Hacker observes, 'Have you noticed how much longer it takes New York buses to get going, since elderly passengers take so much longer boarding and leaving? Or the wait at your bank and post office, when the aged person at the window doesn't understand what he/she is being told?'

The impact of fewer young people

The shrinking of the average family may reinforce the aging of culture. In a world of steadily falling fertility, a growing share of the population will consist of first born and only children. First born children, many social scientists say, are typically more conservative in their social outlook than later-born siblings. According to historian Frank Holloway, 'First borns are less open to innovation, they tend to be more conforming, more traditional and more closely allied with their parents'.

Another possibility is that smaller families may make society less willing to put its young at risk in national emergencies such as war. In past generations, families who lost a son in battle could usually take solace in the survival of his brother, and indeed governments have sometimes exempted only sons from war time service. In the coming decades, will developed societies be willing to place their scarce youth in harm's way to defend national interests?

Peter G Peterson, 'World future society' 19, *The Futurist*, Jan–Feb 2000

Questions 14 to 20

Complete the summary of the first two paragraphs of Reading Passage 2 above. Choose your answers from the box below the summary and write them in boxes 14 to 20 on your answer sheet.

NB   There are more words/phrases or numbers than you will need to fill in the gaps. You may use a word or a phrase more than once.

Summary

The ... (**14**) ... has always looked towards the future because most people were young. The average age of Americans in 1970 was ... (**15**) ..., compared to ... (**16**) ... in developing countries.

In the future, Americans over 30 will form a ... (**17**) ... . It is therefore likely that governments will be more concerned with ... (**18**) ... . In 2030, over 50% of ... (**19**) ... of some countries in Europe and 50% of ... (**20**) ... in America will be over 50 years old.

developed world	the population	all adults	all adults and children
35	18–20	majority	minority
28	special interest group	the aged	developing world

Questions 21 to 26

Choose the letter that most closely describes the author's viewpoint **A–D** for each question and then write the appropriate letter in boxes 21 to 26 on your answer sheet.

21 The aging population …

    A has changed the face of popular culture.

    B will change the type of music we listen to.

    C will mean a rise in pensions.

    D could change the face of popular culture.

22 An aging population may make society …

    A out of touch.

    B risky and changeable.

    C more cultured.

    D remote.

23 According to the author the pace of future society is likely to …

    A speed up.

    B remain the same.

    C become slower.

    D be difficult to predict.

24 The other factor which may age culture is …

    A reduced fertility.

    B the length of time needed to perform simple tasks.

    C more wisdom.

    D an old fashioned education system.

25 First born children are …

    A less willing to take risks in time of national emergency.

    B likely to support their parents views.

    C always more conservative than their siblings.

    D unlikely to be asked to fight in future wars.

26 An aging society is likely to happen …

    A in America.

    B in America and Europe.

    C everywhere.

    D in developing countries.

READING PASSAGE 3

You should spend about 20 minutes on questions 27 to 40.

Short shrift

The benefits of employing part-time staff are well known, but little has been done to improve the quality of, or access to part-time work.

The long awaited consultation document on part-time work had the potential to tackle the long hours culture, underpin the government's family friendly stance and encourage flexibility in the labour market, but the reality is disappointing. Opting for a light touch, the regulations fail to improve the quality of part-time work or to aid the development of part-time work on a voluntary basis.

More than six million people (a quarter of the workforce) work part-time, including nearly one million men. Two categories – wholesale, retail and motor trade, and health and social work account for 45 percent of part-time jobs, with many more in the hospitality industry. The increase in part-time work has been a major feature of employment trends in the past decade, but most jobs remain low-paid and low in status.

Many employers already acknowledge the key role that part-time work plays in employment strategies. Tesco, for example is on record as describing its part-time workforce – which makes up 65% of the total – as the 'lifeblood' of the organisation. Labour supplies can be tailored to trading peaks and demand for ever longer trading hours.

Furthermore, specialist jobs do not always require full-time cover, particularly in smaller organisations. Christine Pointer, a chief executive with a local authority who works with limited budgets, finds it better to employ a more senior professional on a part-time basis, rather than a less qualified person full-time. Part-time work at senior levels also helps to retain key staff who might otherwise leave the organisation.

Unfortunately, not all employers recognise these potential benefits. In the health service for example, where few such opportunities exist, many doctors leave, despite the high cost to the state of training them. And the insurance sector has lower levels of part-time working than any other area of financial services.

Sadly the widespread view that part-time work is primarily attractive to women with caring responsibilities is reinforced both by legislature and organisational culture. The growing trend for men to seek a better work/home balance is being ignored. Women have managed to negotiate limited access to part-time work at senior levels on the back of equal opportunities legislation. But the assumption remains that there is something odd about men who want to work part-time – they lack ambition and commitment to their employer.

Disabled employees represent a large proportion of the workforce that could benefit from part-time work. The labour force identifies over two million economically active people with a long term health problem or disability. It also shows that nearly fifteen million people of working age judge themselves to be covered by the Disabilities Discriminations Act's definition of disability. This includes almost one million who are not working but would like to. For many of them, part-time work is the simplest 'reasonable adjustment' that an employer can make.

On access to training for part-timers, the consultation document again disappoints. While placing an obligation on employers not to exclude part-timers in principle, there is no legal requirement to structure training to accommodate them. New technologies can and do provide flexible access to training – making this omission inexcusable. Ironically, the government is on record as saying that competitiveness depends on the UK making the best use of the talents of as many people as possible and that the larger the number of people to which business can look, the better. However, little is done to encourage the development of these talents in the workforce.

Similarly nothing has been done to alter the perception that part-time work is a 'woman's issue'. A recent press release states 'the new measures will simplify the legal position for part-timers – 80% of whom are women – who will no longer have to go down the indirect route of claiming discrimination under the sex discrimination act'. Wonderful! But occupational segregation is still maintained by gender.

Anna Allan, *People management*, 3 February 2000.

Questions 27 to 32

Choose one phrase **A–I** from the box to complete each of the following key points. Write the appropriate letters **A–I** in boxes 27 to 32 on your answer sheet.

NB There are more phrases than key points so you will not use all of them. You may use any of the headings more than once.

List of phrases
A many of them are voluntary.
B most of them are poorly paid.
C they don't have to provide training at appropriate times.
D if they want to work part-time.
E if they can't work part-time.
F would like to work.
G part-time senior professionals.
H wouldn't be able to work full-time.
I less qualified full-time employees.
J people would prefer to work full-time.
K part-time female employees.
L they don't have to offer training to part-timers.

Example   **Answer**

Many employees   **H**

27 Although there are many more part-time jobs,

28 Often smaller organisations prefer to hire

29 Senior staff might leave the organisation,

30 Men are thought to lack ambition,

31 Nearly one million disabled people

32 Although employers are required not to discriminate against part-timers,

Questions 33 to 40

Using NO MORE THAN THREE WORDS, complete the following statements. Write your answers in boxes 33 to 40 on your answer sheet.

Part-time employees can adapt to ... (**33**) ... better than full time staff.

Many organisations assume that part-time work is only attractive to ... (**34**) ... .

Part-time work is available for women at senior levels because of ... (**35**) ... .

Men who want to work part-time are considered to ... (**36**) ... .

Employers could help ... (**37**) ... to find work by allowing them to work part-time.

New technology has made access to training ... (**38**) ... .

Despite statements to the contrary, part-time work is still seen as a ... (**39**) ... .

The new legislation is designed to make ... (**40**) ... of part-timers clearer.

After you have completed this practice test check the Answer Key.

FOCUSING ON
IELTS
READING
AND
WRITING
SKILLS

UNIT 2: Writing

1 What is in the IELTS writing module?

A comparison of Academic and General Training Writing Modules

		Academic	General training
Format of questions			
Task 1	Different	You are usually asked to describe and interpret in your own words a graph or chart	You are asked to write a letter describing a situation that you are in and requesting someone to do something about it
Task 2	Same	You are asked to give an opinion or suggest a solution to a problem	You are asked to give an opinion or suggest a solution to a problem
Level of difficulty of topic			
Task 1	Different	More difficult	Easier
Task 2	Different	More difficult	Easier
Time allowed			
Task 1	Same	20 minutes	20 minutes
Task 2	Same	40 minutes	40 minutes
Number of words required			
Task 1	Same	150 words	150 words
Task 2	Same	250 words	250 words
Test-taking Tips			
Task 1	Same	See in	See in
Task 2	Same	2 Test-taking tips	2 Test-taking tips
Writing strategies			
Task 1	Same	See in	See in
Task 2	Same	3 The writing strategies you need	3 The writing strategies you need
Writing skills			
Task 1	Different	See in	See in
Task 2	Same	4 The writing skills you need	4 The writing skills you need
Your study program			
Task 1	Different	See in	See in
Task 2	Same	5 Developing your study program	5 Developing your study program

2 Test-taking tips

What should you do when you take the IELTS writing module?

MANAGE YOUR TIME

The test advises you to spend 20 minutes on Task 1 and 40 minutes on Task 2. It is very important that you follow this advice. Here is a suggestion for how to manage your time.

Read

Read the tasks carefully.

Plan

After you understand what is required in the task, then plan what you are going to write. Reading and planning should take about five minutes in Task 1 and Task 2.

Write

After you have planned your writing, begin to write. Writing will take about ten minutes in Task 1 and about 25 minutes in Task 2. Start with Task 2 as it contributes more to your overall band score.

Do not copy the question. Make sure you answer the question asked only.

Check

After you have finished writing, it is important to go back and check your writing. Checking should take about five minutes in Task 1 and Task 2.

Even if you have not completed Task 1 in the recommended time, go on to Task 2. Remember that Task 2 is worth more marks than Task 1.

ACHIEVE THE MINIMUM NUMBER OF WORDS

You have to write the minimum number of words, otherwise you will receive a lower mark.

You do not get extra points for writing more. In Task 1 you should write no more than about 200 words, and in Task 2 no more than about 300 words.

You should practise writing two pieces in 60 minutes. Choose a sample Task 1 and a sample Task 2 from this book. Make sure you write the minimum number of words and use standard A4-size paper.

PRESENT YOUR WRITING WELL

You will write your two tasks on a separate Answer Sheet that you will be given in the test room.

In the IELTS test, you do not receive a mark for your presentation. However, if your writing is difficult to read (for example, written *through* the lines instead of on the lines), the assessment may be more negative.

Crossing out words is perfectly acceptable if you make a mistake.

Practise writing two tasks in 60 minutes, making sure your presentation is as neat and clear as possible.

Ask teachers, schoolmates or colleagues if they have any difficulty in reading your handwriting.

3 The writing strategies you need

How should you write? Being an effective and efficient writer means more than writing accurately (with correct grammar and spelling) and knowing a lot of vocabulary. Both of these things are important, but they do not automatically give you a good mark in the IELTS writing module.

To become an effective and efficient writer:

- first, decide what you will write
- plan your writing
- make sure your writing focuses on the reader
- finally, check your writing.

WRITING IN DIFFERENT WAYS

READ ME

There are different ways to write. What you write will depend on why you are writing and to whom you are writing. When you write, you need to ask yourself these questions: Why am I writing? Who am I writing to/for? What am I writing? What should my writing contain? How should my writing be organised? Are there standard ways of doing that type of writing?

EXAMPLE

	Example A Task 1 (General Training)	Example B Task 2 (Academic)
Why are you writing?	You want to complain about the air-conditioning in your apartment.	You must do a college assignment about the possible future of computer technology.
What are you writing?	You are writing a letter.	You are writing a short report.
To/for whom are you writing it?	You are writing the letter to your landlady.	You are writing the report for your university tutor.
How will you write it?	You will write the letter in semi-formal language, explaining the problem and asking her to take action.	You will write the report in formal language, giving your opinion and supporting it with evidence and examples.

Because examples A and B have different purposes and different audiences, they will produce different kinds of writing (a letter and a report), and the content and structure will also be different.

EXAMPLE

As an example of writing, think of this book. It is written to help people do well in the IELTS test, so its audience is IELTS candidates. It uses semi-formal language and makes the content as clear and as well organised as possible. There are some standard ways of writing this type of book; for example, it must have a list of contents, it must be divided into units and it must provide an answer key.

PLANNING YOUR WRITING

READ ME

Before you start writing, you should first make a plan. You don't get marks for your plan, but having a plan will help make your writing more organised and you do get marks for that.

You make a plan by thinking about the question and deciding what you will write about. Your plan is a list of what you will write, written in a very short way. Some people find it useful to write the plan down on the Question Paper. Do not write your plan on the Answer Sheet. Some people prefer to imagine the plan in their minds. You can decide which way is better for you.

For every task first read the question carefully and then develop a plan. The plan should be like a list. Each point in the list will become a paragraph when you write it up. In this unit you can see examples of plans for each task: Task 1 General Training, pages 76–77; Task 1 Academic, pages 87–88; Task 2 General Training, page 104; and Task 2 Academic, page 104.

FOCUSING ON YOUR READER

READ ME

Whatever you write, you must focus on your reader. You are not writing for yourself. In each writing task in the IELTS test, you are told who you are writing for (for example, a university tutor). This is to test whether you know how to write appropriately as well as how to write accurately. You must use the appropriate 'style', which means using the right type of language for a specific situation, for a specific reader. If you wrote 'Hi! How are you?' in a report you would be using the wrong style. In a report you should:

- Use the full forms of words. Do not use contracted forms, such as *can't*, *I'll*, *don't*, or abbreviations such as *eg*.

- Use standard vocabulary. Do not use slang, such as *kids*.

- Write only about the topic. Do not make personal comments directly to your reader, such as *I hope you like my essay*.

When you write, keep your reader in mind. In the following example read the three sentences and notice that the meaning of each sentence is the same but the style is different because the readers are quite different.

EXAMPLE

A letter to my friend	A letter to my current employer	A report to my new employer
(informal language)	(semi-formal language)	(formal language)
I'm going to quit my job by the end of the year so I can find somewhere to live and new schools for the kids. I reckon I'll be able to start my new job on about January 28th.	*I plan to leave my current job before the end of the year so that I can find new accommodation and schools for my children. I believe I will be able to take up my new position around January 28th.*	*I intend resigning from my current employment prior to the end of the year in order to locate new accommodation and new schools for my children. I should be in a position to commence duty on January 28th.*

In the IELTS test, you must do only what the task tells you to do and no more than that. You must write about a particular topic for a particular reader. Focusing on your reader will help you to make sure that everything you write is relevant. If you don't do what the task tells you to do, you will lose marks. For example, if the task asks you to give your opinion about whether school children should wear uniforms, don't write about taking examinations at school. That is not relevant. If the task asks you to give your opinion about banning smoking, don't write about banning alcohol. That is not relevant and you will lose marks.

CHECKING YOUR WRITING

READ ME

It is important to check your writing while you write and after you have finished writing. Don't be afraid to erase or cross out words.

When you check your writing you need to:

- check the content – is everything clear and relevant?

- check the accuracy of your writing – are the grammar and spelling correct?

- check the presentation – is everything neat and clear?

Develop your grammar skills as much as possible for the IELTS test. Get one or two good grammar reference books and one or two grammar workbooks. Do the exercises in the workbooks without any help. Check the answer key and see where you have made mistakes. Make a list of your problems. Get one or two grammar tests. Do the tests without any help and within a time limit. Check the answer key and see where you have made mistakes. Gradually develop your own personal checklist of grammar points that you think are important and difficult.

RESOURCES

Here is a list of some useful grammar resources:

Coe, N 1995. *Grammar spectrum 3: English rules and practice*. Oxford: Oxford University Press

Hashemi, L and R Murphy 1995. *English grammar in use: Supplementary exercises*. Cambridge: Cambridge University Press

McEvedy, M R 1996. *Learning grammar in context*, rev. ed. Melbourne: Nelson

Murphy, R 1994. *English grammar in use*, 2nd ed. Cambridge: Cambridge University Press

Swan, M 1995. *Practical English usage*, 2nd ed. Oxford: Oxford University Press

Swan, M and C Walter 1997. *How English works*. Oxford: Oxford University Press

---

If you have access to the Internet, you can use a range of search engines to search 'English grammar' and 'English grammar tests'. There are many free grammar resources on-line.

Practise grammar points that are important for the IELTS test. On pages 83 and 116 there is a suggested list of priority grammar for each of the tasks. Use this list to find examples in your grammar references and make sure you understand the grammar points. Find exercises for them in your grammar workbooks and make sure you know how to use them. Continue to do more practice exercises and practice tests.

READ ME

4 The writing skills you need

This section focuses on the skills you need to succeed in the IELTS writing module. First we look at Task 1 General Training and then Task 1 Academic (which are different from each other), and then at Task 2 for both General Training and Academic (where the skills needed are the same for both).

Task 1 General Training and Task 1 Academic both ask you to produce a piece of descriptive writing. General Training candidates have to describe a situation while Academic candidates have to describe what they see in a table or graph.

TASK 1 GENERAL TRAINING: WRITING EFFECTIVE LETTERS

Understanding Task 1

READ ME

What do you have to write in Task 1 and to whom do you have to write?

You must write a letter requesting information or explaining a situation. The letter must contain at least 150 words.

The task will tell you to whom you must write. It may be someone in the general community or someone at university or college, or perhaps an acquaintance or a friend.

Doing Task 1

READ ME

How do you have to write Task 1? You must write in the appropriate style or register for each situation. You must organise your writing in a good standard manner and you must use appropriate language and ideas.

Here is a simple four-step guide to doing Task 1 (General Training).

Steps	Suggested time	Detail
Step 1 Read and understand the task.	2 minutes	Understand the topic. Understand the question. Understand the requirements.
Step 2 Plan what you are going to write.	3 minutes	Plan the letter: greet; state the purpose; give/request information; request action; close and sign off.
Step 3 Write your answer on the Answer Sheet.	12 minutes	Write a greeting. State your purpose. Give/request information. Request action. Close. Sign off.
Step 4 Check your writing.	3 minutes	Check the content. Check the language. Check the presentation.

Now let's look at each of these steps using the sample task below as a model.

Task 1 (General Training)

> You should spend about 20 minutes on this task.
>
> > You rent a house through an agency. The heating system has stopped working. You phoned the agency a week ago but it still has not been repaired.
>
> Write a letter to the agency. Explain the situation and tell them what you want them to do about it.
>
> You should write at least 150 words.
>
> You do NOT need to write your own address.
>
> Begin your letter as follows: *Dear Sir/Madam*

Step 1: Read and understand the task

Suggested time limit: 2 minutes

First read the situation you have to write about. Then read what you have to do and make sure that you understand the requirements of the task.

Details of Step 1	Sample Task 1
Understand the topic.	The topic is: You rent a house through an agency. The heating system has stopped working. You phoned the agency a week ago but it still has not been mended.
Understand the task.	The task is: Write a letter to the agency. Explain the situation and tell them what you want them to do.
Understand the requirements of the task.	You should write at least 150 words. You do NOT need to write your own address. Begin your letter as follows: *Dear Sir/Madam*

Step 2: Plan what you are going to write

Suggested time limit: 3 minutes

After you read the task, develop a plan. A plan is a list of what you will write, written in a very short way. Each point in the list will become a paragraph in your writing.

Some people find it useful to write their plan on the Question Paper. Do not write your plan on the Answer Sheet. Some people prefer to imagine the plan in their minds. You can decide which way is better for you.

Details of Step 2	Plan for sample Task 1
Greet	*Dear …*
State purpose	*Say why I'm writing*
Give/request information	*Give or ask for information to support this*
Request action	*Say what I want done*
Close	*Close*
Sign off	*Yours …*

Step 3: Write your answer on the Answer Sheet

Suggested time limit: 12 minutes

READ ME

You should have a total of four to seven short paragraphs (not counting the greeting and the signing off). Like an essay or a report, your letter has three main sections:

- the introduction – your opening paragraph which states your purpose in writing;

- the body – the paragraphs supporting your purpose; and

- the conclusion – where you request your reader to do something, before closing and signing off.

Your letter must be organised into paragraphs in a clear step-by-step manner, with a logical connection between one idea and the next, one sentence and the next, and between one paragraph and the next.

One way to show this connection is to use a noun or pronoun to refer back to the previous sentence(s), for example: *My heating system is not working and I cannot sleep. This problem is affecting …*

Depending on the topic and the question, it may be possible to organise your points into paragraphs that begin with words such as *Firstly, Secondly, Finally*. Do not, however, organise your writing into a numbered or bulleted list.

Look again at the section on 'reference'. Also, check your grammar references and grammar workbooks (see page 74) for 'reference', and 'cohesion/cohesive devices'.

Write a greeting

You will be told what to write in the greeting. For example, 'Begin your letter as follows: *Dear Sir/Madam*.'

State your purpose for writing

Start writing on the next line after *Dear Sir/Madam*. Tell your reader why you are writing. For example: *I am writing to complain about the heating system in my house*. Or *I am writing about/with regard to the heating system in my house*.

Exercise 1: Stating purpose in a letter (GT)

In a letter, your first line should tell the reader the reason you are writing. For example, when writing a letter to apply for a job:

I saw your advertisement in the paper and I would like to apply for the position of ...

Write the first line of a letter for the following situations.

To a landlord

1 Your airconditioner has stopped working.

_____

2 You will be at least one week late paying your apartment rent.

_____

3 There are rats in the kitchen.

_____

To a language centre

4 You want some information about new courses.

_____

5 You have to return to your country for two weeks.

_____

6 You have lost your certificate and would like the school to send you a copy.

_____

To a friend

7 You are going to study in Australia.

_____

8 You have heard she has won the lottery.

_____

9 You are changing address.

_____

Give/request information

Give and/or request information that will support your purpose. For example, if your purpose is to complain, then complain. For example:

EXAMPLE
I phoned your agency a week ago about this. It has still not been mended. I am very concerned about this.

When you give information, use your imagination to add extra details. The details, however, must be relevant to the task (the situation and the question). If you are having difficulty thinking of enough details (hence enough words), try to ask yourself 'wh-' questions.

Words that begin 'wh-' questions

when   *why*   *what*   *what time*   *who*   *where*

Some of these questions will be relevant to the situation, others will not be relevant.

Sample Task 1 (General Training) gives you the basic information: *You phoned the agency a week ago.* You could ask yourself these 'wh-' questions:

- When did you phone? (I phoned your agency on Thursday 27th January)

- Why did you phone? (I phoned your agency to speak to someone, to complain)

- What did you phone about? (I phoned about the problem with the heating system)

- Who did you phone? (I spoke to one of the staff of the agency)

- What was the result of phoning? (the person said that it would be fixed in two or three days)

So, now we have this sentence with added details:

I phoned your agency on Thursday 27th January and spoke to one of your staff about this problem. She told me that the problem would be fixed in two or three days.

When you give or request information, you can say how you feel about the problem but don't be impolite. For example:

EXAMPLE   I am very concerned/upset/worried about this.

When you request information, you can ask your question directly, for example:

When will the repairman come?

Or you can ask the question indirectly, for example:

I would like to know when the repairman will come.

OR

Could you please tell me when the repairman will come?

The grammar of English questions is quite different from many other languages, so make sure you use grammar references and grammar workbooks to understand and practise these structures (see page 74).

When you give or request information, make sure you write full sentences and paragraphs: Do not write a numbered or bulleted list.

Exercise 2: Requesting information in a letter (GT)

Complete the table using direct and indirect questions to ask about accommodation. There is more than one way of asking the same question.

Accommodation

Topic	Direct questions	Indirect questions
1 size of the rooms	*How big are* _____ _____	*I would like to know* _____ _____
2 cost per week	_____ _____	*Could you please tell me* _____ _____
3 include meals	*Are meals* _____ _____	_____ _____
4 telephone	*Is there* _____ _____	_____ _____
5 separate bathroom	_____ _____	_____ _____
6 number of people in the house	_____ _____	_____ _____
7 distance from public transport	_____ _____	_____ _____

Request action

In this part of the letter you are requesting action, that is, you want your reader to do something, such as fix your heating system, answer your question, respond to an invitation. For example, here are different ways to request the agency to send someone to fix the heating system.

EXAMPLE

Could you please send someone to fix the heating system?

Please fix the heating system.

Could you please fix the heating system?

Would you mind fixing the heating system?

Again, it may be necessary to add details. After thinking about some 'wh-' questions you might add the following details:

Could you please send someone to my house to fix my heating system as soon as possible?

Close

Write on a new line. Depending on the situation, here are some ways to close your letter.

EXAMPLE

Thank you for your attention/for your attention to this matter/for your kindness.

I look forward to seeing you/meeting you/your reply.

Sign off

On a new line write *Yours sincerely* or *Yours faithfully*. For the purposes of the IELTS test, it is not necessary to write your name or your signature.

Here is a complete answer to sample Task 1 (General Training).

SAMPLE

Sample answer

Greet	*Dear Sir/Madam*
State your purpose	*I am writing to complain about a serious problem in my house, which I rent through your agency. The heating system in my house has completely stopped working.*
Give/request information to support your purpose	*This situation is causing many problems for us during this very cold weather. It is affecting my children's study, my husband's work, and my own health.*
Give/request more information to support your purpose	*I telephoned your agency on Thursday 27th January and spoke to one of your staff about the heating system. I explained the situation to her and she told me that the problem would be fixed in two or three days, but in fact nothing has happened. Seven days have now passed and I have not received any communication from your office at all. Naturally I am very concerned about this.*
Request action	*Could you please send a repairman to fix my heating system as soon as possible? It is now urgent.*
Close	*Thank you for your attention to this matter.*
Sign off	*Yours faithfully*

Step 4: Check your writing
Suggested time limit: 3 minutes

READ ME

After you finish writing, you must then check your writing.

- Check the content – have you answered the question and is everything you have written appropriate and relevant to the topic and the question? When you are checking, don't hesitate to erase or cross out words.

- Check the language – are your grammar and vocabulary appropriate and correct? You should know where your potential problems in grammar are. Keep a personal grammar checklist.

- Check the presentation of your writing. Is it neat and clear? Don't hesitate to erase or cross out words and write them again more clearly.

Exercise 3: Checking for relevance (GT)

Read this task.

You should spend about 20 minutes on this task.

> Your telephone has been cut off. It may have been caused by a recent storm. Although you have reported the problem twice, nothing has been done about it.

Write a letter to the telephone company explaining the situation and asking them to repair the line as soon as possible.

You do NOT need to write your own address.

Begin your letter as follows: *Dear Sir/Madam*

You should write at least 150 words.

Now read this sample answer written by a student. Cross out any information that you think is not relevant.

Dear Sir/Madam

I am writing to inform you that our telephone has been out of order for over a week after the recent storm. This has been a major problem as I have been expecting an important call from my sister in Canada who is about to have a baby. Now, I don't know whether the baby has arrived or whether it is a boy or a girl.

I have already telephoned your office twice from a neighbour's phone and both times members of your staff promised to come out and fix the problem within twenty-four hours. The other day I stayed at home all day waiting for your technician to arrive, but he never came. This was particularly inconvenient as I had to take the day off work and my office is very busy at the moment.

Please send a technician as soon as possible. I look forward to hearing from you.

Yours faithfully

Being assessed for Task 1

READ ME Both General Training and Academic candidates are assessed in the same way. You are assessed for:

- task fulfilment
- coherence and cohesion
- vocabulary and sentence structure

Task fulfilment

READ ME This means that you get good marks if you do what the task tells you to do, that is, you write about the topic in an appropriate way for the reader and you give clear and relevant ideas, information and examples to carry out your purpose.

Coherence and cohesion

READ ME

This means that you get good marks if your writing is coherent (it makes sense) and cohesive (it is clearly organised) and so easy for the reader to follow.

Vocabulary and sentence structure

READ ME

You are assessed not only for the *accuracy* of your grammar, vocabulary and spelling, but also for the *range* of your sentence structures and vocabulary.

Accurate grammar and spelling

It is important to make sure that your grammar and spelling are as accurate as possible. See the recommendations for studying grammar on page 74.

The priority grammar points for Task 1 (General Training) are listed in the table below.

EXAMPLE

Grammar point	Examples
Past tense	I'm sorry, I <u>was</u> late yesterday.
	I really <u>enjoyed</u> your party last week.
Present perfect tense	The oven <u>has been broken</u> for over a week.
	I <u>have been studying</u> English for 5 years.
	I <u>have attended</u> university since September.
Present tense	My class <u>starts</u> at 900.
	They <u>have</u> parties every night.
Requests	<u>Would it be possible</u> for me to borrow your notes?
	<u>Could you</u> send me information about the trip?
Question forms	<u>Do you</u> know where he lives?
	<u>What</u> clothes should I bring?
	<u>When</u> does the course start?
Cause and effect	I can't go <u>because</u> it is too expensive.
	It is too expensive <u>so</u> I can't go.
Contrast	He ate four pies <u>but</u> he was still hungry.
	He was always late. <u>However</u>, he got the best test result.

Always choose the structures and vocabulary that you feel confident about. Don't think of what you want to say in your first language and then try to translate it into English. In your first language your structures and vocabulary will be complex and it may be difficult to translate it. Instead, always ask yourself: 'What can I say *in English* that is clear enough and accurate enough?'. For example, if you wanted to say *he is very diligent* but you are not confident about the spelling, it would be better to say *he works very hard.*

Range of vocabulary

READ ME

It is also important to demonstrate that you have a suitable knowledge of vocabulary. You will be judged on the range of your vocabulary. Using a limited range of vocabulary, even if the words are accurate, may not achieve a high mark. At the same time, the vocabulary should be appropriate. If you are writing to a university or a company, for example, your vocabulary should be more formal than if you are writing to a friend.

To understand what is meant by 'more formal', look at the pairs of examples below. In each pair the meaning is the same, but the style is different.

EXAMPLE

Less formal	More formal
She gets good money.	She receives a good salary.
A lot of people are angry about …	Many people strongly disagree with …
People are worried about the environment.	The environment is a major issue.
I'm not really sure, but …	It is possible …
People say …	It is often said …

Range of sentence structures

READ ME

In all languages, people combine what they say into complex sentences. Complex sentences have more than one clause, which means that they have more than one verb. Your writing in the IELTS test is assessed for having a mix of simple sentences and complex sentences. However, don't attempt complex sentences if they are inaccurate or if they make your meaning unclear. It is better to use accurate and clear simple sentences.

You can look at complex sentences in the following exercise.

Exercise 4: Complex sentences (GT)

Read the following passage and answer the questions. All your answers will be complex sentences. This means that each of your answers will have at least two separate verbs. Underline the verbs in each answer.

'Writing an essay in my first language is already difficult, but in the IELTS test I have to do it in English, in a limited time.'
Thai IELTS candidate

Writing can be a very challenging skill especially when you have to write in a foreign language in a university or college environment. The IELTS reflects this challenge by requiring you to complete two pieces of writing within 60 minutes. To be successful, you must plan your pieces of writing quickly and then write them so that they are not only accurate but also appropriate. This unit aims to develop your skills in the standard ways of writing.

… continued over

--- continued

1 What did the candidate say?

Writing an essay in my first language is already difficult, but in the IELTS test I have to do it in English, in a limited time.

2 Is writing a challenging skill?

_____

_____

3 What must you do to be successful?

_____

_____

TASK 1 ACADEMIC: DESCRIBING AND INTERPRETING

Understanding Task 1

READ ME What do you have to write and to whom do you have to write?

In Task 1 (Academic) you must write a short essay or general report of at least 150 words which describes and interprets what you see in a table, graph or diagram.

Usually your essay or report must be written for a course tutor, an examiner or a university lecturer. You are given this information so that you will write in the appropriate formal style. There are examples of formal style on page 84.

Do not worry about the exact meaning of 'tutor', 'examiner', or 'lecturer'. You can think of your audience as teachers. This means that your audience is a typical educated adult. It is not necessary to explain really basic things to them, but other things you can explain because they do not have specialist knowledge.

You do not know the reader and so you must write in an appropriately formal style. In general do not address the reader directly. In your essay or report, do not write the words 'tutor', 'examiner' or 'educated reader', and do not write 'Dear …' as you are not writing a letter. Just begin your essay or report as described on the next page in Step 1.

Doing Task 1

READ ME How do you have to write Task 1? You must write in the appropriate style for each situation. You must organise your writing in a good standard manner and you must use appropriate language and ideas.

Here is a simple four-step guide to doing Task 1 (Academic).

In Steps	Suggested time	Detail
Step 1 Read and understand the task.	2 minutes	Understand the topic by reading the title, the horizontal axis and the vertical axis, or the table headings. Understand the question. Understand the requirements.
Step 2 Plan what you are going to write.	3 minutes	Plan the introduction (summarise the topic, introduce the graph/table). Plan the body (state the main point and other important/interesting points). Plan the conclusion (re-state the main point).
Step 3 Write your answer on the Answer Sheet.	12 minutes	Summarise the topic and introduce the graph/table (the introduction). State the main point and other important/interesting points (the body). Re-state the main point/s (the conclusion).
Step 4 Check your writing.	3 minutes	Check the content. Check the language. Check the presentation.

Now let's look at each of these steps using the sample task below as a model.

SAMPLE

Sample Task 1 (Academic)

You should spend about 20 minutes on this task.

The graph below shows the different modes of transport used to travel to and from work in one European city in 1950, 1970 and 1990.

Write a report for a university lecturer describing the information shown below.

You should write at least 150 words.

… continued over

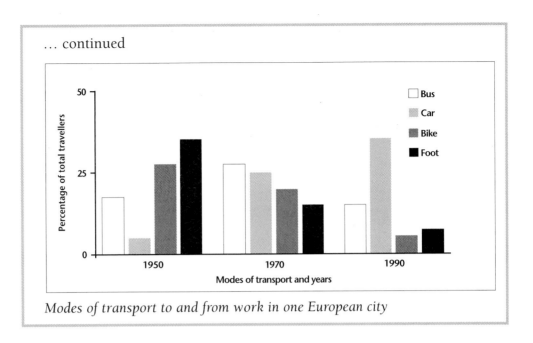

... continued

Modes of transport to and from work in one European city

Step 1: Read and understand the task
Suggested time limit: 2 minutes

READ ME   First read the topic. Then read what you have to do and make sure that you understand the requirements of the task.

Details of Step 1	Sample Task 1
Understand the topic.	The topic is: The graph shows the different modes of transport used to travel to and from work in one European city in 1950, 1970 and 1990.
Understand the task.	The task is: Write a report for a university lecturer describing the information shown on the graph.
Understand the requirements of the task.	You should spend about 20 minutes on this task. You should write at least 150 words.

Remember that reading a table or graph is the same as reading a passage. You need to locate the title and skim over everything to get a general idea. Then, if it is a graph, scan more specifically for the information contained in the horizontal axis and the vertical axis. If it is a table, scan more specifically for the information contained in the table headings.

Step 2: Plan what you are going to write
Suggested time limit: 3 minutes

READ ME   After you read the question, develop a plan. A plan is a list of what you will write, written in a very short way. Each point in the list will become a paragraph in your writing.

Some people find it useful to write their plan on the Question Paper. Do not write your plan on the Answer Sheet. Some people prefer to imagine the plan in their minds. You can decide which way is better for you.

Details of Step 2	Plan for sample Task 1
Plan the introduction	*Summarise topic (modes of transport to and from work)*
	Introduce data (the bar chart)
Plan the body	*State main point (major change in use of cars)*
	State other important/interesting points (fall in number of people walking/cycling; change in use of buses)
Plan the conclusion	*Re-state main point*

Step 3: Write your answer on the Answer Sheet
Suggested time limit: 12 minutes

Summarise the topic and introduce the table or graph

READ ME Start writing on the first line. Do not write the question or give your essay/report a title. Start by introducing the topic. To do this, write a summary sentence saying what the table or graph is about. For example:

EXAMPLE *People* in this city use four modes of transport to travel to and from work: bus, car, bike and foot.

Then tell your reader what information you have on this topic. What specifically does the graph or table show? To help you with this, look at the horizontal axis and the vertical axis of the graph or the headings on the table. For example:

The *graph* indicates the percentage of total travellers who used these four modes of transport in 1950, 1970, and 1990.

You can use the words given in the task, for example, *The graph shows the …* but it is better to say this in a slightly different way in your own words.

State the main point and other important/interesting points

Identify a point that you think is very important. If you were telling a friend about what you read in the graph what would you say? For example, you might select the increase in the use of cars as a main point. For example:

EXAMPLE There was a major change in the use of cars.

OR

Cars become much more popular during the period 1950 to 1990.

It is not necessary to explain the data in the IELTS test, for example, why car travel increased. Here is a possible paragraph:

The most significant change occurred in the use of cars. In 1950 only about 5% of travellers used a car to go to and from work, but this rose to 25% in 1970 and to over 35% in 1990.

Then describe other important, interesting or unusual points. It is not necessary to describe all of the data in the graph or table. Generally each point will be a separate paragraph, but sometimes you may combine several points together in one paragraph.

The central section or body of your report will usually contain two to four short paragraphs. For example:

EXAMPLE

Another striking change involves travelling on foot. In 1950 about one in three people walked to and from work, but this fell to around 20% in 1970 and to a very low 5% in 1990.

Travelling by bike also fell dramatically, while bus travel first increased and then declined, although in 1990 it was the second most popular type of transport.

Re-state the main points

Conclude your report by re-stating your main point. When you re-state, try to use slightly different words. There are many phrases you can use in your conclusion.

Phrases that introduce conclusions				
To conclude	*In conclusion*	*To summarise*	*In summary*	*In general*

Here is a sample conclusion.

EXAMPLE

In general it can be said that in the period 1950 to 1990 the use of cars to travel to and from work increased dramatically, while other forms of transport either remained constant or declined.

Here is a complete answer to sample Task 1 (Academic).

SAMPLE

Sample answer

The introduction: Summarise the topic and introduce the graph/table.	*People in this city use four modes of transport to travel to and from work, namely bus, car, bike, and foot. The graph indicates the percentage of total travellers who used these four modes of transport in 1950, 1970, and 1990.*
The body: State the main point and other important and interesting points.	*The most significant change occurred in the use of cars. In 1950 only about 5% of travellers used a car to go to and from work, but this rose to 25% in 1970 and to over 35% in 1990.*
	Another striking change involves travelling on foot. In 1950 about one in three people walked to and from work, but this fell to around 20% in 1970 and to a very low 5% in 1990.
	Travelling by bike also fell dramatically, while bus travel first increased and then declined, although in 1990 it was the second most popular type of transport.
The conclusion: Re-state the main point/s.	*In general it can be said that in the period 1950 to 1990, the use of cars to travel to and from work increased dramatically, while other forms of transport either remained constant or declined.*

Classifying, comparing, showing relationships and describing trends

READ ME When you do Task 1 (Academic) you may need to classify, compare, show relationships, and describe trends and quantities.

Classify

You may have to classify the information you see in the table or graph. For example:

EXAMPLE
- There are four different types/kinds/categories/varieties of X. (*There are four different modes of transport: bus, car, bike and foot.*)

   OR

- X can be divided/classified into four different types/kinds/categories/varieties. (*Modes of transport can be divided into four kinds: bus, car, bike and foot.*)

Compare

READ ME When you describe a table or graph, you often need to compare information. The next exercise presents an example of a graph that compares.

Exercise 5: Reading graphs that compare (A)

Which of the following graphs (A, B or C) accurately presents the information in the following sentence?

In 1990 the average price was $15 per unit, but this had risen to over $20 by 1995.

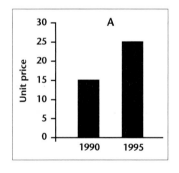 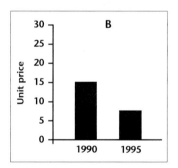 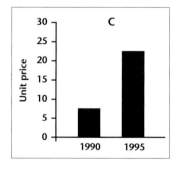

Show relationships

READ ME Sometimes a writer uses graphs and tables to *show a relationship*. The writer is saying that there is a connection (or 'correlation') between two kinds of information ('factors' or 'variables'). For example, in graph 1 in the next exercise, the writer is showing that there is a correlation between how heavy minor voles are when they are born and how long they live. It is not possible, however, for the writer to argue that one factor is the cause of the other. For example, the writer cannot say that low birth weight causes earlier death, unless of course other evidence is available apart from the graph.

Look at the graphs and answer the questions.

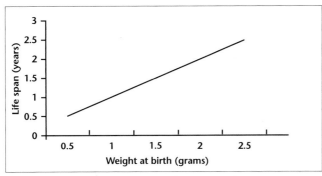

Life span and birth weight of minor voles

1 What is this graph doing?

It is expressing the relationship between weight of minor voles at birth and life span. It is implying (suggesting) that there is a connection between the two, that the lower the birth weight, the shorter the life span.

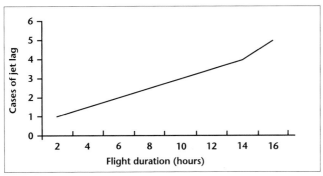

Flight duration and reported cases of jet lag

2 What is this graph doing? _____

_____

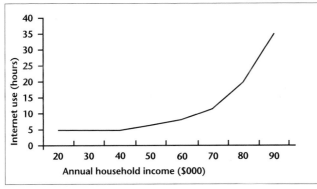

Annual household income and Internet use

3 What is this graph doing? _____

_____

Describe trends

READ ME When you compare something across two or more points of time, then you are able to *describe a trend*. In Task 1 (Academic) you can usually use the simple past tense because you are describing what happened between two points of time. For example, between 1995 and 2000 something *changed* or *rose*, or *decreased* or *fell*. The present perfect tense is less likely, but you should know how to use it. The present perfect tense describes what has happened between a point of time and now. For example, from 1990 until now something *has changed, has risen*, or *has decreased/has fallen*.

Subject	Past tense verb	Adverb
The price The population The rate	decreased, fell, declined, went down, dropped	*how* quickly? gradually/slowly quickly/rapidly
	increased, rose, grew, went up	*how* much? slightly somewhat significantly/substantially dramatically
	remained, stayed	steady/constant/stable

If you use this structure throughout the task your writing becomes repetitive. One way of changing the structure is to use a noun, for example: *There was a dramatic fall in the price.* This alternative structure is shown in the following table.

There was	a	adjective	noun	in noun
There was	a	gradual/slow/rapid slight/significant/ substantial/dramatic	decrease/fall/decline/ drop/increase/rise	in prices in the population in the rate

The vocabulary that writers use to describe trends is important. Check the words in this vocabulary list and memorise them. When you find other similar words, add them to this list.

Words to describe trends

to increase; an increase	*to rise (rose/risen); a rise*	*to soar*
to plunge	*to plummet*	*to tend; a tendency*
sharply	*significantly*	*slightly*
to level out; a level	*to stabilise*	*steady*
a trend	*a pattern*	*to grow; growth*
to decline; a decline	*to fall (fell/fallen); a fall*	

Exercise 7: Describing trends (A)

Look at the list on the previous page. Describe what happened to these things in your country during the period 1980 to 2000. Use the words and structures given in the two tables above.

1 divorce rate

_____

2 average age at marriage

_____

3 birth rate

_____

4 exchange rate of local currency (against $US)

_____

5 literacy rate

_____

6 population

_____

7 pollution in major cities

_____

8 price of computers

_____

9 income tax rates

_____

10 life expectancy

_____

11 cost of living

_____

12 average income

_____

READ ME   Look again at the vocabulary you can use to compare and to describe trends (page 92). Also check that you know the prepositions that go with these verbs and nouns. For example:

EXAMPLE
- The rate remained (steady/constant) at 30 points.
- In 1980 the rate stood at 30 points.
- The rate increased by 10 points from 30 points in 1950 to 40 points in 1970.
- The rate fell/dropped by 10 points from 40 to 30.
- There was an increase in the rate of 10 points from 30 to 40.
- There was a drop/a fall in the rate of 10 points from 30 to 40.

Exercise 8: Describing trends (A)

Describe the changes in this man's weight and height during the period 1980 to 2000. Use words from the two tables on page 92.

Man	1980	1990	2000
weight (kg)	44	62	69
height (cm)	135	178	178

1 _____

2 _____

Describe quantities

Tables and graphs usually *describe quantities*, that is, amounts and numbers. To describe what you see, you need to practise words that specify the quantity of a noun, such as *the majority of* people or *most* people. Here is a list of words you can use, from the highest amount to the lowest amount.

> **Words that specify quantity**
>
> *all   almost all   the vast majority   the majority   many   most*
>
> *a lot   quite a lot   some   quite a few   a few   only a few   a little*
>
> *only a little   only a minority   a minority   almost no   no (none)*

Exercise 9: Describing quantities (A)

Answer the questions using words like the following:

> all   almost all   the vast majority   the majority   many   most   a lot
>
> quite a lot   some   quite a few   a few   only a few   a little   only a little
>
> only a minority   a minority   almost no   no (none)

1 How many people in your country eat rice every day?

The majority of people in my country eat rice every day.

2 How many people in your country can speak English fluently?

_____

3 How many people in your country are unemployed?

_____

4 How many people in your country watch football on television?

_____

5 How many people in your country read a newspaper every day?

_____

6 How many people in your country go on holiday to other countries?

_____

7 How many people in your country own a computer?

_____

8 How many people in your country go to the cinema regularly?

_____

READ ME When describing graphs and tables you sometimes also need to use words that specify something about a *number*, such as *around* 80%. Here is a list of words you can use, from the highest amount to the lowest. Check the meaning of these words.

Words that specify numbers

well over   slightly over/more   over   approximately   around

about   slightly under/less   under   well under

Exercise 10: Describing numbers (A)

Look at the graph and answer the questions using words like:

well over   slightly over/more   over   approximately   around

about   slightly under/less   under   well under

1 How many patents were applied for in 1900?

_____

2 How many patents were granted in 1917?

_____

3 How many patents were granted in 1933?

_____

4 How many patents were applied for in 1947?

_____

5 How many patents were applied for in 1980?

_____

6 How many patents were applied for in 2000?

_____

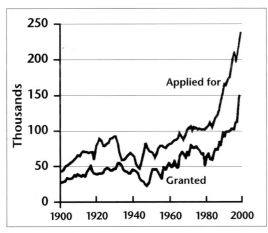

Patent applications

Source: US Patent and Trademark Office

READ ME   It is possible that Task 1 (Academic) will ask you to compare two or more graphs or tables. Use the same steps as when you are reading only one table or graph. In the following exercise you can practise comparing three graphs.

Exercise 11: Comparing graphs (A)

You should spend about 20 minutes on this task.

The graphs show farm size compared to gross output in three countries.

Write a report for a university lecturer comparing the information shown in the graphs.

You should write at least 150 words.

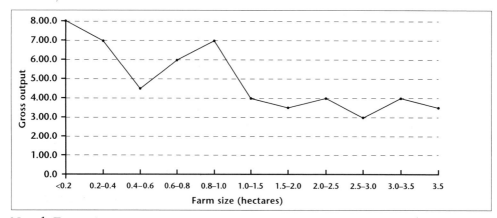

Nepal: Farm size vs gross output

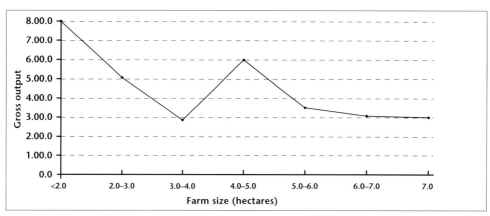

South Korea: Farm size vs gross output

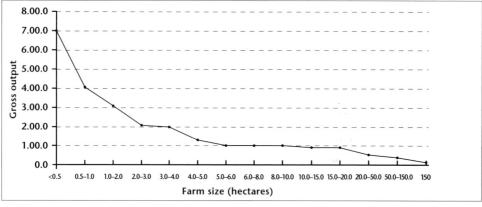

Syria: Farm size vs gross output

Describing processes

READ ME It is possible that Task 1 (Academic) will give you a diagram or flow-chart that shows a *process*. You must describe the process, that is, describe the number of steps in that particular sequence. To describe a process, you can tell your reader what to do by using the imperative form of the verb, such as *Make copies* or by using structures like *You must make copies*. You can also tell your reader what is done in the process by using the passive voice, such as *Copies are made*. To show the sequence of the steps clearly, use words like *first, then, after, once* and *before*.

EXAMPLE For example, the process described in the following sentence can be expressed as a flow-chart.

The harvested grain is <u>first</u> washed and <u>then</u> dried <u>before</u> being ground.

Grain processing

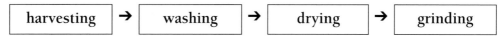

Exercise 12: Describing a process

Complete the diagram according to the information in the sentence.

After all the ballots are collected, they are keyed into the computer, and then checked by a supervisor before being filed.

Ballot processing

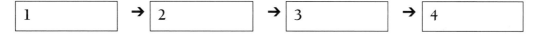

You should spend about 20 minutes on this task.

The diagram below shows a company's recruitment process.

Write a report for a university lecturer describing this process.

You should write at least 150 words.

```
                    ┌─────────────────────┐
                    │  List of requirements │
                    │     is drawn up       │
                    └──────────┬──────────┘
                               │
                               ▼
                    ┌─────────────────────┐
                    │ Advertisement is placed │
                    │   in the newspaper    │
                    └──────────┬──────────┘
                               │
                               ▼
                    ┌─────────────────────┐
                    │   Applicant asks for  │
                    │   application form    │
                    └──────────┬──────────┘
                               │
                               ▼
                    ┌─────────────────────┐
                    │ Applicant completes and │
                    │ returns application form │
                    └──────────┬──────────┘
                               │
                               ▼
                    ┌─────────────────────┐
            ┌───────┤ Application opened    ├───────┐
            │       │   and assessed        │       │
            │       └─────────────────────┘       │
            ▼                                       ▼
  ┌──────────────────┐                  ┌──────────────────┐
  │ Application rejected │                │ Applicant invited for │
  │                    │                  │    an interview     │
  └─────────┬────────┘                  └─────────┬────────┘
            │                                       │
            ▼                                       ▼
  ┌──────────────────┐                  ┌──────────────────┐
  │    Letter sent     │                  │     Interview      │
  └──────────────────┘                  └─────────┬────────┘
                                        ┌──────────┴──────────┐
                                        ▼                      ▼
                            ┌──────────────────┐   ┌──────────────────┐
                            │ Successful applicant and │ │ Application rejected │
                            │  runner up selected   │   │                    │
                            └─────────┬────────┘   └─────────┬────────┘
                                      │                      │
                                      ▼                      ▼
                            ┌──────────────────┐   ┌──────────────────┐
                            │ Successful applicant │  │    Letter sent     │
                            │   offered the job    │  │                    │
                            └──────────────────┘   └──────────────────┘
```

Step 4: Check your writing

Suggested time limit: 3 minutes

READ ME

After you finish writing, you must then check your writing.

- Check the content – have you answered the question and is everything you have written appropriate and relevant to the topic and the question? When you are checking, don't hesitate to erase or cross out words.

- Check the language – are your grammar and vocabulary appropriate and correct? Be aware of your potential problems in grammar. Use your personal grammar checklist when you check your writing. Look at the spelling of words. Remember: it is acceptable to erase or cross out words so that you can change them.

- Check the presentation of your writing. Is it neat and clear? Don't hesitate to erase or cross out words and write them again more clearly.

You can practise checking for relevance in the following exercise.

Exercise 14: Checking for relevance (A)

Read this task.

You should spend about 20 minutes on this task.

The bar chart shows the unemployment rates by sex and birthplace in Victoria.

Write a report for a university professor describing the information shown in the bar chart.

You should write at least 150 words.

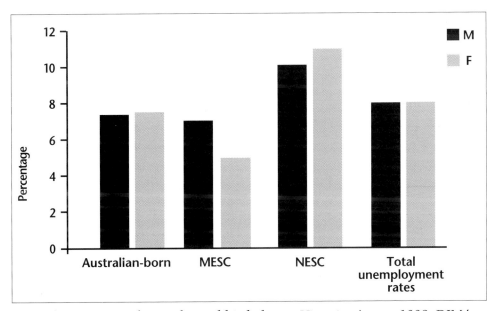

Unemployment rates by gender and birthplace – Victoria, August 1998, DIMA

Legend: MESC = Main English Speaking Countries
NESC = Non English Speaking Countries

… continued over

... continued

Now read this sample answer written by a student. Cross out any information that you think is not relevant.

The chart illustrates the unemployment rates for Victoria in August 1998. The bars represent the person's sex and where they were born.

The highest percentage of unemployed were born in non-English speaking countries. This is not surprising as it is very difficult to find a good job when you have to use a foreign language. Perhaps the government should offer free language training courses to migrants before they leave their own country.

It is interesting to note that migrants from main English-speaking countries are more likely to find work than people born in Australia. This could mean that Australian people are lazy or that the migrants have particularly useful skills. The chart also shows that fewer women (4%) from main English-speaking countries are unemployed, whereas in general the unemployment rates for men and women are about the same (8%).

In conclusion an overall unemployment rate of 8% is still too high. The government of Victoria must create more jobs so that everyone has a chance to work.

Exercise 15: Describing tables (A)

You should spend about 20 minutes on this task.

The table below shows the number of overseas students enrolling in language schools in Australia between 1996 and 1998 and the geographical areas from where they come.

Write a report for a university lecturer describing the information shown in the table.

You should write at least 150 words.

Nationality	1996	1997	1998
Asian	64 841	59 857	43 220
European	6 695	8 012	4 378
Central and South American	839	1 392	1 345
African	–	126	499
Total	72 534	69 387	49 442

Total enrolments 1996, 1997 and 1998

Being assessed for Task 1

READ ME   Both Academic and General Training candidates are assessed in the same way. See pages 82–85 for a full description. You are assessed for:

- task fulfilment
- coherence and cohesion
- vocabulary and sentence structure

The priority grammar points for Task 1 (Academic) are:

Grammar point	Examples
Past tense	The rate of inflation rose last year.
Comparisons	Sales figures were higher in 1986 than in 2000.
Prepositions of time/ prepositions used with numbers	Sales increased <u>in</u> June. Sales stood <u>at</u> 92 in April. There was an increase <u>of</u> 10 points. Sales increased <u>by</u> 10 points.
Quantifiers	Sales increased <u>slightly</u>. Sales increased <u>significantly</u>.
Structures describing trends	The price rose rapidly. There was a rapid rise in the price.

TASK 2 GENERAL TRAINING/ACADEMIC: STATING YOUR POINT OF VIEW

READ ME   Task 2 (General Training) and Task 2 (Academic) are very similar. The only difference is the type of topic.

In the Academic module, the topics are somewhat more academic, that is, they are topics of general interest that people at university and college might discuss.

In the General Training Module, the topics are more general, that is, they are the topics of general interest that people in the general community might discuss.

Note that the topics are of general interest in both cases and it makes no difference what subjects candidates study. It is reasonable to say, however, that the Academic topics are more difficult than the General Training topics. Still, the format of the tasks is the same and the skills required are the same.

Understanding Task 2

READ ME   What do you have to write in Task 2 and for whom do you have to write?

In Task 2 you must write a short essay or general report in which you state your point of view. Usually your essay or report must be written for a course tutor, an examiner or a university lecturer. You are given this information so that you will write in the appropriate formal style. There are examples of formal style on page 84.

Do not worry about the exact meaning of 'tutor', 'examiner', or 'lecturer'. You can think of your audience as teachers. Another possible audience is an educated reader with no specialist knowledge. This means that your audience is a typical educated adult. It is not necessary to explain really basic things to them but other things you can explain because they do not have specialist knowledge.

You do not know the reader and so you must write in an appropriately formal style. In general do not address the reader directly. In your essay or report, do not write the words 'tutor', 'examiner' or 'educated reader' and do not write 'Dear ...' as you are not writing a letter. Just begin your essay or report as described below in Step 1.

Doing Task 2

How do you have to write Task 2? In Task 2 you must argue, that is, you must present an opinion. In this type of writing, you express your opinions and give reasons to support your opinions. Sometimes you also predict what might happen in the future.

You must write in the appropriate style or register for each situation. You must organise your writing in a good standard manner and you must use appropriate language and ideas.

Here is a simple four-step guide to doing Task 2.

In Steps	Suggested time	Detail
Step 1 Read and understand the task.	5 minutes	Understand the topic. Understand the question. Understand the requirements.
Step 2 Plan what you are going to write.	5 minutes	Plan the introduction (state your view). Plan the body (support your view). Plan the conclusion (re-state your view).
Step 3 Write your answer on the Answer Sheet.	25 minutes	State your view (the introduction). Support your view with reasons, arguments, examples (the body). Re-state your view (the conclusion).
Step 4 Check your writing.	5 minutes	Check the content. Check the language. Check the presentation.

Now let's look at each of these steps using the sample tasks following as models.

Sample Task 2 (General Training)

> You should spend about 40 minutes on this task.
>
> As part of a class assignment you have to write about the following topic.
>
> > Some businesses now say that no one can smoke cigarettes in any of their offices.
> >
> > Some governments have banned smoking in all public places.
> >
> > This is a good idea, but it also takes away some of our freedom.
>
> Do you agree or disagree? Give reasons for your answer.
>
> You should write at least 250 words.

Sample Task 2 (Academic)

You should spend about 40 minutes on this task.

Present a written argument or case to an educated reader with no specialist knowledge of the following topic.

> It is inevitable that as technology develops so traditional culture must be lost. Technology and tradition are incompatible – you cannot have both together.

To what extent do you agree or disagree with this statement?

You should write at least 250 words.

Step 1: Read and understand the task

Suggested time limit: 5 minutes

First read the topic. Then read what you have to do and make sure that you understand the requirements of the task.

Details of Step 1	Sample Task 2
Understand the topic.	The topics are: • Some businesses now say that no one can smoke cigarettes in any of their offices. Some governments have banned smoking in all public places. This is a good idea but it takes away some of our freedom. • It is inevitable that as technology develops so traditional cultures must be lost. Technology and tradition are incompatible – you cannot have both together.
Understand the task.	The tasks are: • Do you agree or disagree? Give reasons for your answer. • To what extent do you agree or disagree with this statement?
Understand the requirements of the task.	You should spend about 40 minutes on this task. You must write for your class teacher/an educated reader. You should write at least 250 words.

Step 2: Plan what you are going to write

Suggested time limit: 5 minutes

READ ME

After you read the question, develop a plan. The plan is a list of what you will write, written in a very short way. Each point in the list will become a paragraph in your writing.

Look at the following two examples of a plan.

EXAMPLE

Details of Step 2	Plan for sample Task 2 (General Training)
The introduction	*State viewpoint:* *Smoking should be banned.*
The body	*Support this viewpoint:* *Reason 1: the dangers to smokers and non-smokers, financial loss.* *Reason 2: smokers can still smoke in certain areas, banning smoking good for public health.*
The conclusion	*Re-state viewpoint:* *Banning smoking excellent idea, won't take away freedom.*

EXAMPLE

Details of Step 2	Plan for sample Task 2 (Academic)
The introduction	*State viewpoint:* *Strongly disagree, technology and tradition are compatible.*
The body	*Support this viewpoint:* *Argument 1: in many countries they live side by side, eg Japan.* *Argument 2: throughout history technology incorporated into traditional cultures, eg introduction of tractors.* *Argument 3: technology can preserve traditional cultures, eg ancient manuscripts, artifacts.*
The conclusion	*Re-state viewpoint:* *Traditional cultures not necessarily lost through development of technology.*

Step 3: Write your answer on the Answer Sheet
Suggested time limit: 25 minutes

READ ME
Your essay or report should contain four to five paragraphs:

- the introduction – the first paragraph
- the body – two to three paragraphs
- the conclusion – the final paragraph

Don't write 'introduction', 'body' and 'conclusion' in your writing but remember them as a guide.

In some countries people have a different structure when they write. For example, they give some background information first, then they give some relevant arguments, and then they state or imply their viewpoint. This is a valid way to structure writing but it is not recommended for the IELTS writing module.

State your viewpoint

READ ME
Do not write the question and do not give your essay or report a title. Start by stating your viewpoint directly. For example:

> I completely agree/disagree with this statement. I believe/do not believe that smoking should be banned in all offices and in all public places and I agree/disagree that this takes away some of our freedom.

Sometimes the question will ask you to what extent you agree. You can respond to this by saying, for example: *I totally/completely/strongly agree/disagree.*

You can also say that you *partly agree*. Arguing in this way is acceptable, but it can be more complex because it requires you to compare. In general, it is easier and safer to say that you *totally/completely/strongly agree/disagree.* In this way, you can argue clearly.

Remember, though, that you might have to argue both sides of the issue. For example, you might have to explore both the advantages and the disadvantages of something.

Sometimes you might have to predict the future. For example, the question might be: *In the future there will be a world government, do you agree?* Your viewpoint might be something like: *I believe that the world will improve greatly in the future.*

In order to predict, the area of grammar you need to practise is modal auxiliary verbs (modals) of possibility. For example: *The world may/might/could/will improve.*

Also check some of the vocabulary that can be used to introduce your predictions.

Phrases that introduce predictions

I am/am not sure/certain that …	*I feel confident/quite confident that …*
I believe/do not believe that …	*I anticipate/do not anticipate that …*

You can practise predicting in the following exercise.

Exercise 16: Predicting (GT/A)

Look at the list below. What do you think will happen to these things in your country during the next 20 years?

1 divorce rate

_____

_____

2 average age at marriage

_____

_____

3 birth rate

_____

_____

4 exchange rate of local currency
(against $US)

_____

_____

5 population

_____

_____

6 literacy rate

_____

_____

7 pollution in major cities

_____

_____

8 price of computers

_____

_____

9 income tax rates

_____

_____

10 life expectancy

_____

_____

11 cost of living

_____

_____

12 average income

_____

_____

READ ME   After you have stated your viewpoint, then introduce your reasons for having this opinion. The statement of viewpoint and the introduction of the reasons together form the introduction to your essay or report. For example:

EXAMPLE   I completely disagree with this statement. I believe that smoking should be banned in all offices and in all public places and I do not believe that this takes away some of our freedom. There are two main reasons why I hold this view.

If you have to discuss both sides of an issue, then you might say something like:

There are both advantages and disadvantages to this approach.

Support your viewpoint

READ ME   You have stated your opinion. When you are planning your writing, you also need to state reasons that support your viewpoint. Use your own ideas, knowledge and experience.

The reasons you give can be an argument, for example:

EXAMPLE

People do not have the right to damage the health of other people.

and/or an example, such as:

We are simply limiting the location of this activity, just as we limit the places where we can all urinate, for example.

The body of your writing should contain two to four paragraphs. Usually you need a separate paragraph for each reason. Here are some ways of introducing each paragraph.

Introducing paragraphs in the body of your essay		
A paragraph containing a reason (an argument and/or an example) why you have that viewpoint	Firstly ...	One reason for this (opinion/viewpoint) is that ...
A paragraph containing another reason (an argument and/or an example) why you have that viewpoint	Secondly ...	In addition ...
A paragraph containing another reason (an argument and/or an example) why you have that viewpoint	Thirdly/ Finally ...	Another reason for this opinion/viewpoint is that ...

Remember that the aim of your writing is to show what you can do with English. It is not to show who you are or how clever you are. Let's say you are writing about your opinions on school uniforms. In fact you are opposed to them, but you can think of better arguments and better vocabulary in favour of them. What should you do? Choose what will give you a better performance in English and argue in favour of them!

Don't try to translate your ideas. Don't ask yourself: What can I say about this topic? Instead, ask yourself: What can I say about this topic *in English*? With this approach, you will choose the structures and vocabulary that you can say in English with reasonable confidence that they will be correct. What you write will not be as complex or sophisticated as what you can write in your first languages, but it will be correct and clear, and it will get a good mark. Trying to translate could result in a lot of errors, which means you will get a low mark.

Look at the example of argumentative writing on the next page. It shows the stages that a writer goes through when giving and supporting an opinion for an IELTS task.

EXAMPLE

The issue	What should we do about the traffic?
The writer expresses her viewpoint about this issue. She proposes a suggestion. She draws a conclusion.	I think we can improve the traffic problem by improving public transport. The government should build an underground train system.
She puts forward arguments to support her claim.	Many people would leave their cars at home and use the train if it were reliable and cheap. Improving public transport is more efficient and better for the environment.
She quotes evidence to support her claim.	The government's own surveys in 1997 concluded that over 20% of people would use a new train system regularly.
She argues against someone else's claims.	I don't agree with the government that we must build roads to solve the traffic problem. More roads will lead to more cars.

Words in argumentative texts

an opinion   a fact   a viewpoint   a stance   a position

to argue for/in favour of   to argue against   to put forward an argument

to claim   to make a claim   to support   to prove   to imply

to indicate   to show

evidence   an implication

to conclude   to draw a conclusion   to come to a conclusion

You can practise supporting viewpoints in the following exercise. Here you must explore both sides of the issue, looking for arguments in favour of the proposal and arguments against it.

Exercise 17: Arguing (GT/A)

Find as many arguments as you can to support and reject the following statements.

Statement	For	Against
School uniforms should be abolished in all schools.	• uniforms are expensive so not having to buy them saves money • children can be more individual	• uniforms reduce inequality • uniforms teach discipline
Smoking cigarettes should be made illegal.		
It is better to be beautiful than rich.		
Shops should be open 24 hours a day.		
Mobile phones are not good for society.		

The following Exercises 18 and 19 also focus on supporting viewpoints.

Exercise 18: Seeing how writers support their viewpoints (GT/A)

Read the following letter written to a newspaper and then answer the questions.

I have lived near Foxley Woods for over forty years and I strongly believe the proposed bypass is not only unnecessary but would destroy the unique character of the area.

Traffic has managed to find its way through the village of Greystoke with the minimum of delay throughout my life. Why is there now this sudden need for a new road? The other day I carried out an experiment: I drove on the existing road from Blacksheep Dip to Greystoke, a journey supposedly of some ten kilometres, in exactly four and a half minutes. What is more I made this journey at 5.30 on a Friday afternoon in the so-called rush hour. If the existing road is not fast enough, how fast do the council want us to go?

Foxley woods is one of this country's few remaining patches of virgin woodland. It is home to a number of rare species including Harvey's elephant mouse, the grey-headed shrike and the lesser shrew. If the bypass is built these animals will have their habitat disturbed and will run the danger of ending up as road kill. Not only this but new roads bring development, so in all likelihood our woods will soon end up as part of a housing estate.

We must stand together and fight this ill begotten barbaric plan.

1 What is the main point of the letter?

_____

_____

2 What are the topic sentences for paragraphs 2 and 3?

Paragraph 2:_____

Paragraph 3:_____

3 What arguments/evidence does the writer use to support each topic sentence?

Paragraph 2:_____

_____

Paragraph 3:_____

_____

4 What action does the writer propose?

_____

Read this task.

You should spend about 40 minutes on this task.

> Due to the influence of world-wide media such as television and computers, the gap between cultures is narrowing. The introduction of this 'global culture' is of great benefit to the world.

To what extent do you agree with this viewpoint?

You should write at least 250 words.

Now read this sample essay.

The international mass media has for the first time resulted in the majority of people sharing the same experiences. Films such as Titanic *are known the world over and musicians and sports stars are celebrated all over the world. Many people believe this common ground brings people closer together.*

Another advantage of a global culture is that issues such as human rights become internationalised. It is much harder for a country to keep abuses hidden, when foreign television crews bring atrocities into the living rooms of the world.

However, global culture does have disadvantages. The media tends to be concentrated in a few hands, so the public doesn't get a balanced perspective. News broadcasts often represent the viewpoint of the owner rather than an objective opinion. Although global culture has its advantages, it is often bland and without any real value. This is because it needs to appeal to the widest range of viewers possible and so has to try to find a product that will keep everyone happy.

Media tycoons' main aim is to make money and so it is easier to rely on marketing gimmicks rather than make a product of lasting value. At the same time, businessmen are more concerned with markets than morals and so will not air controversial stories for fear of offending the local government. Therefore, global culture tends to be a watered down international product designed to appeal to the lowest common denominator.

Although a global culture offers some advantages, the nature of business dictates that this potential is rarely fulfilled.

Write a plan for the essay. Include:

1 an introduction

2 arguments giving the advantages of global culture

3 supporting evidence for these arguments

4 arguments against global culture

5 supporting evidence

6 a conclusion re-stating the writer's view

Re-state your viewpoint

In your final paragraph, conclude your essay or report by re-stating your view. It is also a good idea to refer back to your reasons. For example:

> For these reasons, I strongly believe that a ban on smoking in all offices and public places is an excellent idea that will not take away anyone's freedom.

When you re-state, try to use slightly different words. For example: if in your first paragraph you wrote *I completely disagree with this statement*, then in your last paragraph you could write something like *I strongly believe that …*

Here is a complete answer to sample Task 2 (General Training).

Sample answer (General Training)

> You should spend about 40 minutes on this task.
>
> As part of a class assignment you have to write about the following topic.
>
>> Some businesses now say that no one can smoke cigarettes in any of their offices. Some governments have banned smoking in all public places. This is a good idea but it takes away some of our freedom.
>
> Do you agree or disagree? Give reasons for your answer.
>
> You should write at least 250 words.

The introduction: State your view.	*I completely disagree with this statement. I believe that smoking should be banned in all offices and in all public places and I do not agree that this takes away some of our freedom. There are two reasons why I hold this view.*
The body: Support your view with reasons, arguments, examples.	*Firstly, giving smokers the 'freedom' to smoke in offices and public places is very dangerous, both for the smokers themselves and for the people near them. Perhaps people should have the right to kill themselves slowly, but this causes a financial loss to our community, since we all pay either directly or indirectly for the health costs associated with smoking. However, smokers certainly do not have the right to damage the health of other people. The 'freedom' to hurt other people is not a genuine freedom.*
	Secondly, the ban on smoking in offices and public places does not actually threaten anyone's freedom. People may continue to smoke. We are simply seeking to limit the location of this activity, just as we limit the places where we can all urinate, for example. We do this for the same reason in both cases, namely public health. Few people would think that their freedom is

… continued over

… continued

limited because they cannot urinate in offices or public places. Why do they then complain when businesses and governments try to protect people from the health dangers associated with passive smoking?

The conclusion:
Re-state your view.

For these reasons, I strongly believe that a ban on smoking in all offices and public places is an excellent idea that will not take away anyone's freedom.

Here is a complete answer to sample Task 2 (Academic).

SAMPLE

Sample answer (Academic)

You should spend about 40 minutes on this task.

Present a written argument or case to an educated reader with no specialist knowledge of the following topic.

It is inevitable that as technology develops so traditional cultures must be lost. Technology and tradition are incompatible – you cannot have both together.

To what extent do you agree or disagree with this statement?

You should write at least 250 words.

The introduction:
State your view

I strongly disagree with this statement. There are several compelling arguments in support of the view that technology and tradition are indeed compatible.

The body:
Support your view with reasons, arguments, examples

Firstly, we can today see many countries around the world where tradition and new technology live side by side very comfortably. Japan, for instance, is a leader in technology but still strongly holds its traditional values, such as respect for elders. Whether Japanese people post hand-written letters to their parents or send them e-mails, the traditional values remain unchallenged and unchanged, although the technology has changed.

Secondly, there are innumerable cases throughout history where we can see that a change in technology did not actually lead to a change in traditional culture. For example, when farmers all around the world started using tractors instead of animals to plough their fields, their productivity and lifestyle improved, but there was no significant change in their behaviour, beliefs and customs. The technology was incorporated into their traditional culture without challenging it.

Finally, we know that technology can actually help

… continued over

... continued

> *preserve traditional cultures. It not only aids us to preserve ancient manuscripts and artifacts and to understand the roots of culture by exploring history. It also helps with communication, and communication is the basis of all culture. Communication devices such as satellite televisions and cellular telephones are, for example, of great benefit to geographically scattered cultures. Improved telecommunications technology enhances the ability of these cultural groups to stay in touch with one another and find ways of safeguarding their culture.*

The conclusion:
Re-state your view

> *For these reasons, it is easy to support the view that technology and tradition are indeed compatible. As technology develops, traditional cultures are not necessarily lost.*

Step 4: Check your writing
Suggested time limit: 5 minutes

READ ME   After you finish writing, you must then check your writing.

- Check the content – have you answered the question and is everything you have written appropriate and relevant to the topic and the question? When you are checking, don't hesitate to erase or cross out words.

- Check the language – are your grammar and vocabulary appropriate and correct? Be aware of your potential problems in grammar. Use your personal grammar checklist when you check your writing. Look at the spelling of words. Remember: it is acceptable to erase or cross out words so that you can change them.

- Check the presentation of your writing. Is it neat and clear? Don't hesitate to erase or cross out words and write them again more clearly.

You can practise checking for relevance in the following Exercises 20 and 21.

Read this task.

You should spend about 40 minutes on this task.

As part of a class assignment you have to write about the following topic.

> Soon it will be scientifically possible to clone humans. What are the advantages and disadvantages of this?

You should write at least 250 words.

Now read this sample answer written by a student. It contains some irrelevant information. Underline any sentences that are not relevant to the question.

Over the past hundred years modern science has advanced faster than ever before. One hundred years ago people were only just starting to use electricity and hadn't discovered antibiotics. Now they have the Internet and will soon be able to clone human beings.

Many people disagree with cloning because they feel that the world is already facing problems of overpopulation without copying the people who are already alive. There are enough people born today without creating extra mouths to feed. It has also been said that scientists will use cloning to duplicate famous leaders and that this technology could be very dangerous if it got into the wrong hands. I once saw a film where evil scientists cloned Hitler and tried to take over the world. What is more, countries may try to make a master race or a population that only has qualities that the government considers desirable.

There are also some advantages to cloning. Many couples are desperate to have children but are unable to have children naturally. It may be that cloning is the answer. Cloning could also be used to create spare parts for surgery. Therefore if you needed a heart transplant, you would not have to wait for someone to die in a car crash, but just be given a spare heart cloned in the organ bank.

Overall, there are advantages and disadvantages to cloning, so scientists should think very carefully before cloning humans.

Exercise 21: Checking for relevance (A)

Read this task.

You should spend about 40 minutes on this task.

Write a report for an educated non-specialist audience for or against the following topic.

> Over the past fifty years sport has played an increasingly important role in our society as a substitute for war. Therefore the vast amounts of money spent on international competitions such as the Olympic Games can be justified.

You should write at least 250 words.

Now read this sample answer written by a student. It contains some irrelevant information. Underline any sentences that are not relevant to the question.

Major sporting competitions are followed by countries all over the world and in many ways tournaments such as the Olympic Games and the World Cup have taken the place of war as a major source of patriotism. There has not been a major war for the past fifty years and some people argue that this is due to the closer ties established between countries through international sport.

Sport is so important because small countries such as Holland in soccer or Kenya in athletics can become a major focus of international attention. Of course this attention is not always positive, for example when Ben Johnson got banned in the 1988 Olympics for taking drugs. Throughout the world newspapers and news programs devote a lot of time and space to sports news and results. It can be argued that following a country's progress on the sporting field has replaced the need to fight other countries in battle. It is interesting to note that although Manchester United is popular throughout the world many people in Britain hate them.

The 2000 Olympics are being held in Sydney and the World Cup will take place in Korea and Japan. Lots of money has been spent on developing a new stadium for the Olympics and providing accommodation for the athletes and spectators. Money will also be spent on advertising the event all over the world to try to encourage people to buy tickets. Moreover governments have been sponsoring training programs for athletes for many years in order that they might win medals in the games. These training programs are not cheap.

Sport is important because it is a matter of interest to large numbers of people and is a source of national pride for many countries. Everybody hopes that the Olympics and the World Cup will be a great success and that their country will win.

Being assessed for Task 2

READ ME Both Task 2 (General Training) and Task 2 (Academic) are assessed in the same way. You are assessed on arguments, ideas, and evidence; communicative quality; and vocabulary and sentence structure.

Arguments, ideas and evidence

READ ME You get good marks if you fulfil the task by giving clear and relevant ideas, information and examples to support your viewpoint.

Communicative quality

READ ME You get good marks if you state your viewpoint clearly and organise your writing in a clear step-by-step manner that is easy for the reader to follow.

Vocabulary and sentence structure

READ ME You get good marks for correct grammar, range of sentence structures, correct vocabulary, range of vocabulary, and correct spelling.

You are assessed not only for the *accuracy* of your grammar and vocabulary, but also for the *range* of your grammar and vocabulary.

Accurate grammar and spelling

READ ME It is important to make sure that your grammar and spelling are as accurate as possible.

Always choose the structures and vocabulary that you feel confident about. Don't think of what you want to say in your first language and then try to translate it into English. In your first language your structures and vocabulary will be complex and it may be difficult to translate it. Instead, always ask yourself: 'What can I say *in English* that is clear enough and accurate enough?'. For example, if you wanted to say *She is a university lecturer* but you are not confident about the spelling, it would be better to say *She teaches at university*.

The priority grammar points for Task 2 (General Training) and (Academic) are:

Grammar point	Examples
Present tense	I get up at 9.00.
Past tense	I got up at 10.00 yesterday.
Cause and effect	He was late because he missed the bus. He missed the bus so he was late.
Contrast	He didn't work hard but he still passed the test. Although he didn't work hard, he passed the test.
First and second conditional	If it rains tomorrow, I'll stay at home. If I saw a ghost I would take a photograph.
Modals of obligation	I have to start work at 9.00. You mustn't copy your answers from your friend.
Modals of possibility	He might be on holiday. She must have been hungry.
Relative clauses	The man who stole my wallet looked just like you.
Subordinate clauses	You didn't say that you were going on holiday.
Comparisons	He is much taller than me.

Range of vocabulary

READ ME It is important to demonstrate that you have a suitable knowledge of vocabulary. Your writing should contain vocabulary that is appropriate for university or college. This means more formal vocabulary and no slang. At the same time, you must also make sure that the vocabulary you choose is accurate. It is better to use a narrow range of vocabulary correctly than to attempt a wider range of vocabulary that is incorrect.

Look at the pairs of examples below. In each pair, the meaning is the same but the style is different. There are also some examples on page 84.

There are also some examples on page 84.

SAMPLE

Less formal	More formal
They really had a great time.	They really enjoyed themselves.
We can't tell you the results.	The results are confidential.
You're not allowed to write notes.	Notes are not acceptable.
I've got to go to a doctor.	It is essential that I consult a physician.

Range of sentence structures

READ ME

In all languages, people combine what they say/write into complex sentences. Complex sentences have more than one clause, which means that they have more than one verb. This is an effective and efficient way to communicate, and writing at university or college should contain a mix of simple sentences and complex sentences. Your writing in the IELTS test should try to do the same.

You can practise forming complex sentences in the following exercise.

Exercise 22: Complex sentences (GT/A)

For 1 to 5 below, combine the sentences into one sentence. There is more than one possible answer.

1 I love using computers. I still don't own one.

I love using computers although I still don't own one.

2 I want to study information technology. It is expanding rapidly. I think it will lead to good jobs.

_____

3 I am planning to study at Dulacca University. It is a leading centre for computer studies.

_____

4 I will have to study several subjects. They are all new to me.

_____

5 I am really looking forward to studying. It will be quite difficult.

_____

READ ME

Check your grammar references and grammar workbooks for 'complex sentences', 'compound sentences', 'relative clauses' and 'subordinate clauses'. You are looking for ways to combine information into complex sentences.

Words to use when combining simple sentences

and   or   but   although   where   when   before   while   as   since

because   who (whom/whose)   that   which

At the same time, you must also make sure that the structures you choose are *accurate*. It is better to use simple sentences correctly than to attempt complex sentences that are incorrect.

5 Developing your own study program

To prepare for the IELTS writing module you need to devise a study program that will help you develop your writing strategies and writing skills.

READ ME

- First decide what your needs are.
- Then choose some writing topics that you can use for practice.
- Then practise the strategies and skills required by the writing module.

DECIDING YOUR NEEDS

READ ME

Think about what you need. Do you need, for example, to focus on expanding your vocabulary? Do you need to practise writing complex sentences? Do you need to check your understanding of what is in the writing module? Complete the following checklist to help you to think about your needs.

Writing checklist	(✔)
Do you know what is in the writing module?	( )
Do you know:	
how long the writing module lasts?	( )
how many tasks there are?	( )
the formats of the tasks?	( )
how many words you must write?	( )
Do you know what skills you need to improve in your writing?	( )
Do you need to improve:	
your planning skills?	( )
making your writing organised and connected?	( )
focusing on your reader and making your writing more relevant?	( )
making your grammar accurate?	( )
using a mix of complex and simple sentences?	( )
making your vocabulary accurate?	( )
using a range of appropriate vocabulary?	( )
checking your writing?	( )
presenting your writing?	( )
Do you have a study plan to develop your writing skills?	( )
Do you write English every day?	( )
Are you learning new vocabulary every day?	( )
Can you state ten new words that you have learned in the past week?	( )
Do you try different exercises when you write?	( )

FINDING APPROPRIATE PRACTICE TASKS

READ ME

Choosing topics that you find interesting is important. If your practice writing is enjoyable, you will probably write more often and that's good for your writing skills!

Like any other skill, the ability to write a foreign language requires a lot of regular practice, especially if your goal is to be able to write accurately and quickly. As a general guideline, you should do at least 30 minutes of focused writing every day. As your study program progresses, you should practise more specific exercises as suggested below.

Task 1 (General Training)

READ ME

Here is a list of practice tasks for Task 1 (General Training). Remember to read and plan first, then write and check. Remember how you will be marked.

1   You have been invited to stay with friends for the weekend. You're not sure how to get to their house, you're not sure what clothes to bring and you're worried that they may have forgotten that you're a vegetarian.

Write a letter accepting the invitation. You would also like to remind your friends that you are a vegetarian.

2   Your telephone has been cut off. You think the problem may have been caused by a recent storm. Although you have reported the problem twice, nothing has been done about it.

Write a letter to the telephone company, explaining the situation and asking them to repair the line as soon as possible.

3   You bought a pair of shoes from a local shop. A week later you noticed that the shoes had holes in them. When you took the shoes back to the shop with the receipt the shop assistant was rude and refused to change them.

Write a letter to the manager of the shop complaining about the service you received and asking for a refund.

4   Your pen pal is going on holiday to your country. He/she has written to you asking about life in your country. He/she would particularly like to know about things to buy, where to stay and what to see.

Write a letter answering his/her enquiries.

5   You have two weeks holiday next month. You saw an advertisement for a package holiday and would like further information.

Reply to the advertisement asking about cost, duration and student discount. You would also like to know some details about the accommodation offered.

6   You were involved in a minor car accident and were forced to miss your lecture this morning.

Write a letter to your lecturer apologising for missing the lecture. Explain what happened and ask if you can have a copy of the notes from the lecture.

7   You get a foreign language magazine delivered to your house by the local newsagency. Over the past six months deliveries have become very irregular.

The last magazine you received was four months old. The subscription is expensive and you are angry about the situation.

Write to the newsagent explaining the situation and cancelling your subscription.

8   A few days ago you lost your wallet on the bus. This morning you received a package from the bus driver containing your wallet.

Write a letter to the bus driver thanking him for his honesty and consideration.

9   You have a part-time job in a shop. You would like to take the next two weeks off because you need the time to revise for your exams. You are willing to take this time as unpaid leave or as part of your holiday entitlement.

Write a letter explaining the situation to your boss.

10   A few months ago you started a course in economics. You have found that you are not really suited to this course and would like to change to a computing major.

Write a letter to the head of the economics faculty explaining the situation.

To create more practice tasks, use your imagination. Think of the kinds of situations people are in when they live in a city environment, especially in an English-speaking environment. This may include situations, issues and problems arising from studying, being at university/college, living on campus, living off-campus, working, transport, shopping, and pursuing hobbies, interests and leisure activities. Generate some practice tasks using this table to help you.

Write a letter to:	• a language school	• complaining about	• the cost of something you bought
	• a university	• describing	• a recent accident you had
	•	•	•
	•	•	•
	•	•	•
	•	•	•
	•	•	•

Task 1 (Academic)

READ ME   To create practice tasks for Task 1 (Academic), you will need to locate suitable tables, graphs and diagrams. Look in high school or university textbooks in such subjects as business, accounting, mathematics, science and engineering, and in business magazines and newspapers that use a lot of tables and graphs.

Task 2 (General Training)

READ ME   Here is a list of practice tasks for Task 2 (General Training). Remember to read and plan first, then write and check. Remember to organise your writing into an introduction, a body and a conclusion and make sure that everything you write is relevant.

1   The best measure of success is how much money you earn.

    To what extent do you agree with this statement?

2   It is better to live a short exciting life rather than a long uneventful one.

    To what extent do you agree with this statement?

3   Soon it will be scientifically possible to clone humans.

    What are the advantages and disadvantages of this?

4   Guns don't kill people, people do. Everyone should have the right to own a gun to protect themselves.

    To what extent do you agree with this statement?

5   Many developing countries are kept in debt by the demands of Western governments.

    Do you agree that Western governments should write off debts owed by the world's poorest nations?

6   Modern technology may make it unnecessary for most people to work in the future.

    Do you agree or disagree with this statement?

7   Hunting animals for fun is wrong.

    Do you agree?

8   People usually make friends who are similar to them.

    Do you agree?

9   In the future, most children will be taught by computer.

    Do you agree?

10 Nowadays people do not have the same respect for their elders as they once had.

    Do you agree?

Task 2 (Academic)

READ ME   Here is a list of practice tasks for Task 2 (Academic). Remember to read and plan first, then write and check. Remember to organise your writing into an introduction, a body and a conclusion and make sure that everything you write is relevant.

1   Government's role is to control society as a whole, not to look after the individual. Therefore everyone should pay for his or her own needs.

    Do you think governments are responsible for the welfare of the individual?

2   Even though it may be scientifically possible in the future for people to live to 200 years old, it is not in the world's best interests for them to do so.

    What are the advantages and disadvantages of people living to 200?

3 Over the past fifty years sport has played an increasingly important role in our society as a substitute for war.

   Can the vast amounts of money spent on international competitions such as the Olympic Games be justified?

4 One of the problems with society today is that many of the best paying jobs are harmful or of no benefit to the majority of humankind.

   To what extent do you agree with this statement?

5 Governments spend large amounts of money on art that ordinary people don't understand. This money could be better spent on things that benefit the majority of the population.

   Do you agree?

6 As global warming has become a reality, the major concern of industry must be the impact of its products on the environment.

   What is the best way for countries to control fossil fuel emissions and other sources of greenhouse gases?

7 Nowadays children as young as ten are committing terrible crimes such as murder and rape. If children commit such crimes age is no excuse and they should be sent to prison for the rest of their lives.

   Do you agree?

8 Children should enjoy their childhood. Therefore they should not be under constant pressure to achieve better results at school.

   Do you agree?

9 There are too many people on this planet so it is logical to look for other planets that humankind can colonise.

   Do you agree that space exploration is the answer to over population?

10 Some people say that the Internet is bringing people together by making the world smaller.

   Do you believe that the Internet is making it easier for people to communicate with each other?

To create more practice tasks, you will need to look in magazines and newspapers. Look at the headlines, the stories, the letters to the editor, and the editorials. Specify the topic (usually an opinion about an issue, problem or event) and then ask a question such as *Do you agree or disagree?*

PRACTISING THE SKILLS NEEDED FOR THE WRITING MODULE

Exercises for independent study

READ ME   Whenever you write, practise all of the writing strategies and skills presented in this unit, for example: making your writing *organised*, making your writing *relevant*, and using a mix of *simple* and *complex sentences*, to name just a few. Practise writing and reading as often as possible.

You should also begin a program of vocabulary development, aiming to learn five to ten new words a day. This is important not only for your reading but also for your writing, speaking and listening. Expanding your vocabulary should be one of the main aims of your study program. You can do this by reading as much as possible. Choose articles that you find interesting in newspapers, magazines, encyclopedias and textbooks. Good writers are usually good readers.

Exercises with study partners

READ ME

Here are some exercises you can do with a partner.

Select a practice Task 1 for your partner (General Training or Academic)

Select a practice Task 1 (see page 121) and give it to your partner. Your partner must write a full answer (150 words) within the time limit of 20 minutes. Evaluate the answer by looking at pages 82–85. Then ask your partner to select or devise a task for you.

Select a practice Task 2 for your partner (General Training or Academic)

Select a practice Task 2 (see pages 122–123) and give it to your partner. Your partner must write a full answer (250 words) within the time limit of 40 minutes. Evaluate the answer by looking at pages 115–118. Then ask your partner to select or devise a task for you.

Use the Internet

Access the Internet to seek pen pals, discussion groups and chat groups in your areas of interest: for example, sports, chess, music, reading. Writing in this way will help the general development of your writing.

6 IELTS practice tests: Writing

IELTS practice test: Writing (General Training)

TIME ALLOWED: 60 MINUTES

Writing Task 1

You should spend about 20 minutes on this task.

You have just bought a new wardrobe from a mail order company. Unfortunately when it arrived you found that one of the doors was missing. You would like the company to come and replace your wardrobe one afternoon next week.

Write a letter to the company asking them to come and collect the wardrobe and replace it with a new one.

You should write at least 150 words.

(After you have completed this practice test check the Answer Key for a sample answer.)

NOTES

Writing Task 2

You should spend about 40 minutes on this task.

As part of a class assignment you have to write about the following topic.

In the future natural resources such as coal and oil will be used up. How can we save on resources? What alternative forms of energy are available?

You should write at least 250 words.

(After you have completed this practice test check the Answer Key for a sample answer.)

NOTES

IELTS practice test: Writing (Academic)

TIME ALLOWED: 60 MINUTES

Writing Task 1 (A)

You should spend about 20 minutes on this task.

The figure shows the percentage of employees in each occupation absent from work for at least one day in a reference week in 1999 due to injury or illness.

Write a report for a university lecturer describing the information shown below.

You should write at least 150 words.

(After you have completed this practice test check the Answer Key for a sample answer.)

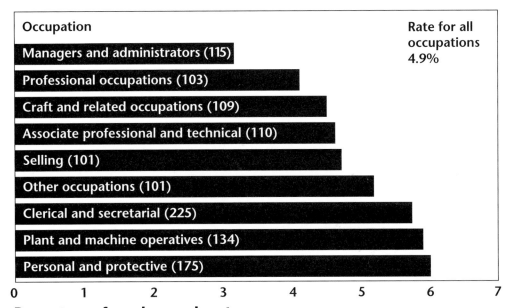

Occupation	Rate for all occupations 4.9%
Managers and administrators (115)	
Professional occupations (103)	
Craft and related occupations (109)	
Associate professional and technical (110)	
Selling (101)	
Other occupations (101)	
Clerical and secretarial (225)	
Plant and machine operatives (134)	
Personal and protective (175)	

Percentage of employees absent

(Figures in brackets equal number of employees counted)

'Labour market trends', National Statistics
© Crown Copyright 2000

NOTES

Writing Task 2

You should spend about 40 minutes on this task.

Present a written argument or case to an educated reader with no specialist knowledge of the following topic.

The world is consuming natural resources faster than they can be renewed. Therefore it is important that products are made to last. Governments should discourage people from constantly buying more up to date or fashionable products.

To what extent do you agree with the statement above?

You should write at least 250 words.

(After you have completed this practice test check the Answer Key for a sample answer.)

NOTES

Answer key

UNIT 1: READING

NOTE: ‖ means alternative possible answers

Example questions	1 A; 2 C; 3 organisms; 4 conception; 5 maximum; 6 females; 7 120 years; 8 4000 years; 9 female; 10 E; 11 A; 12 C
Exercise 1	1 Libraries are quite difficult to define. Libraries are organised in three ways. Nowadays libraries are under threat for a number of reasons. It is difficult to predict the future of libraries.
Exercise 2	2 (5); 3 (10); 4 (14)
Exercise 3	1 journals ‖ newspapers ‖ CD-ROMs ‖ microfilm ‖ audiovisual materials; 2 three; 3 hardware and personnel costs; 4 (as) physical places
Exercise 4	2 1887; 3 (about) one million (people); 4 Brazil ‖ Japan ‖ China (must have two); 5 China; 6 western; 7 adjectives
Exercise 5	1 B; 2 B; 3 D
Exercise 6	2 T; 3 F; 4 NG; 5 T; 6 F; 7 NG; 8 F
Exercise 7 *Sample answer*	An <u>inspection</u> of the skin can <u>reveal alterations such as extreme</u> dryness, growths, ulcers and discolouration. The breasts, prostate, and genitals are palpated to <u>detect</u> tumours, and endoscopic <u>examination</u> of the rectum and colon <u>may be appropriate</u> in <u>older persons</u>. (These words are the least specialised.)
Exercise 8 *Sample answer*	<u>How</u> do we <u>humans produce speech</u>? <u>First</u> the <u>brain issues</u> a <u>command</u> to the <u>lungs</u> to <u>initiate</u> an airstream. <u>Before this</u> airstream <u>can become</u> speech, <u>however</u>, it <u>must pass through, or by</u>, the larynx, pharynx, <u>tongue</u>, <u>teeth</u>, <u>lips</u> and <u>nose – all of which</u> can <u>modify</u> the airstream <u>in various ways</u>. (These words are the least specialised.)
Exercise 9	1 False; 2 A; 3 *Sample answers:* **a** being very overweight; **b** decreasing; **c** too much
Exercise 10	1 True; 2 A; 3 *Sample answers:* **a** harmful; **b** frequency
Exercise 11 *Sample answers*	A A library is a place where books and other materials are kept. B A refrigerator is an electrical appliance that provides cold storage. C A widow is a woman whose husband has died. D A fax machine is a machine that transmits and prints out information over a telephone line.
Exercise 12	1 A tuk-tuk is a motorised three-wheeled vehicle. 2 Culture shock is a feeling of strangeness and discomfort. 3 A polyglot is a person who speaks many languages.

4 The Great Depression was the period of economic collapse in the late 1920s and early 1930s.

5 A leptospermum is an attractive, low-growing tea-tree suited to garden beds or containers.

6 **A** pesticides; **B** a pesticide/a chemical agent used to control pests; **C** Bordeaux mixture

Exercise 13	**1** green tea; **2** oolong tea; **3** black tea
Exercise 14	**1** stooped labour; **2** assembly-line work; **3** sweatshop work
Exercise 15	B
Exercise 16	**1** (1); **2** (4); **3** (2)
Exercise 17	**1** C; **2** C; **3** A
Exercise 18	**1** the locals; **2** No, not likely.
Exercise 19 *Sample answers*	**1** died; **2** she passed the exam

Exercise 20	**1** the emigration of highly-skilled persons
	2 medical workers || engineering workers || business workers || professional workers (any two)
Exercise 21	**cause/effect:** 4, 5, 8, 9; **effect/cause:** 2, 3, 6, 7
Exercise 22	A
Exercise 23	C
Exercise 24	A 3; B 1; C 4; D 2
Exercise 25	A 4; B 2; C 1; D 3
Exercise 26	**1** A 1; B 3; C 4; D 2
	2 A
Exercise 27	A 2; B 3; C 1
Exercise 28	A 5; B 1; C 3; D 4; E 2
Exercise 29	**1** 25; **2** risen

Exercise 30

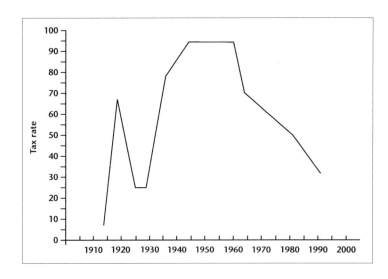

Age	3 years	4 years	5 years
Number	1 041 000	1 772 000	3 157 000
% of same age group in the community	28.9%	49%	86.7%

Enrolment in preschool programs by age group, 1986

Exercise 32

1 cafes; 2 cafes; 3 Poles; 4 at a cafe; 5 young people in Poland;
6 forms of entertainment; 7 people with children; 8 people with children

Exercise 33

1 (flows) of illegal immigrants; 2 some countries; 3 employers;
4 three million illegals

Exercise 34

Sample answers

1 a this pen; b the pen in my hand; c this red pen;

2 a most people; b people who play sport; c friendly people;

3 a all tests; b tests that my teacher gives me; c long tests

Exercise 35

1 F; 2 F; 3 T; 4 NG; 5 F

Exercise 36

Sample answers

1 I do my homework in my bedroom..

2 I do my homework in the evening.

3 I don't like doing homework.

4 I eat while I am doing my homework.

Exercise 37

1 T; 2 F; 3 F; 4 NG; 5 NG

Exercise 38

1 T; 2 F; 3 F; 4 T; 5 F

Exercise 39

1 NG; 2 T; 3 F

Exercise 40

1 T; 2 F; 3 NG; 4 T; 5 NG

IELTS practice test: Reading (General Training)

1 A; 2 A, D; 3 H; 4 B; 5 C, H; 6 C; 7 E, G; 8 D; 9 E, H;
10 G; 11 C; 12 G, H; 13 F; 14 A; 15 D; 16 A; 17 C; 18 C;
19 B; 20 (iii); 21 (x); 22 (ix); 23 (viii); 24 (v); 25 (ii); 26 A;
27 D; 28 G; 29 F; 30 E; 31 N; 32 Y; 33 Y; 34 Y; 35 N;
36 NG; 37 Y; 38 Y; 39 NG; 40 Y

IELTS practice test: Reading (Academic)

1 (ii); 2 (vi); 3 (ix); 4 (v); 5 (i); 6 (x); 7 (iv) 8 N; 9 NG;
10 Y; 11 Y; 12 NG; 13 NG; 14 developed world; 15 28; 16 18–20;
17 majority; 18 the aged; 19 the population; 20 all adults; 21 D;
22 A; 23 C; 24 A; 25 B; 26 B; 27 B; 28 G; 29 E; 30 D;
31 F; 32 C; 33 trading peaks || demand; 34 women;
35 equal opportunities legislation;
36 be odd || lack ambition || lack commitment; 37 disabled people || employees;
38 flexible; 39 woman's issue; 40 the legal position

UNIT 2: WRITING

Exercise 1

Sample answers

1   I am writing to tell you that my airconditioner has stopped working.

2   I am sorry to have to tell you that I will be at least a week late with my rent.

3   I am writing to inform you that there are rats in the kitchen.

4   I am writing to ask for some information about your new courses.

5   I am writing to ask your permission to be absent for two weeks.

6   I am writing with regard to my end of course certificate.

7   I've got some big news to tell you.

8   Congratulations on your big win.

9   I just want to let you know my new address.

Exercise 2

Direct questions	Indirect questions
How big are the rooms?	I would like to know how big the rooms are.
How much does it cost per week?	Could you please tell me how much it costs per week?
Are meals included?	I would like to know if meals are included.
Is there a telephone?	Could you tell me if there is a telephone?
Do I have my own bathroom?	I would like to know if I have my own bathroom.
How many people are in the house?	Would you mind telling me how many people are in the house?
How far is the nearest bus stop?	Could you please tell me how far the nearest bus stop is?

Exercise 3

The following is not relevant:

… from my sister in Canada who is about to have a baby. Now, I don't know whether the baby has arrived or whether it is a boy or a girl.

Exercise 4

2   Writing <u>can be</u> a very challenging skill, especially when you <u>have to write</u> in a foreign language in a university or college environment.

3   To be successful, you <u>must plan</u> your pieces of writing quickly and then <u>write</u> them so that they <u>are</u> not only accurate, but also appropriate.

Exercise 5

A

Exercise 6

Sample answers

2   It is expressing the relationship between flight duration and reported cases of jet lag. It is implying (suggesting) that there is a connection between the two, that the longer the flight, the more reported cases of jet lag there are.

3   It is expressing the relationship between annual household income and Internet use. It is implying (suggesting) that there is a connection between the two, that the higher the annual household income, the higher the Internet use.

Exercise 7	1	The divorce rate rose steadily.
Sample answers	2	The average at marriage increased slightly.
	3	The birth rate fell sharply.
	4	The exchange rate against the US dollar remained constant.
	5	The literacy rate decreased slightly.
	6	The population went up gradually.
	7	Pollution levels grew dramatically.
	8	The price of computers fell sharply.
	9	Income tax rates remained stable.
	10	Life expectancy increased slightly.
	11	The cost of living went up significantly.
	12	Average income remained constant.

Exercise 8	1	The man's weight rose substantially from 44 kg in 1980 to 62 kg in 1990. Between 1990 and 2000 his weight increased by a further 7 kg.
Sample answers	2	He grew significantly from 135 cm in 1980 to 178 cm in 1990. His height remained constant from 1990 to 2000.

Exercise 9	2	Not many people can speak English fluently.
Sample answers	3	Quite a lot of people are unemployed.
	4	Quite a few people watch football.
	5	Most people read a newspaper every day.
	6	Only a few people go on holiday regularly to other countries.
	7	Not many people own a computer.
	8	Quite a lot of people go to the cinema regularly.

Exercise 10	1	Slightly less than 50 000 patents were applied for in 1900.
Sample answers	2	Approximately 50 000 patents were granted in 1917.
	3	Just over 50 000 patents were granted in 1933.
	4	Around 75 000 patents were applied for in 1947.
	5	About 100 000 patents were applied for in 1980.
	6	Slightly under 250 000 patents were applied for in 2000.

Exercise 11
Sample answer

The three graphs compare farm size and gross output in Nepal, South Korea and Syria.

All three countries show that the highest gross output is found on the smallest farms. However, it is important to note that farms in Nepal are much smaller at 0.2 hectares than the farms in the other two countries.

Both South Korea and Nepal show similar trends in output. Crop yield becomes smaller the larger the farm becomes. One interesting aspect of these two graphs is that from 0.4 to 1.00 hectare in Nepal and from 3.00 to 5.00 hectares in South Korea output becomes more efficient before gradually declining as the farms get bigger.

Syria has a far greater spread of farm sizes ranging from under 0.5 of a hectare to over 150 hectares. Output in Syria declines much more rapidly than in the other two countries. Output falls from 7.00 for farms of less than 0.5 hectares to just over 0.10 for farms of over 150 hectares.

Overall output seems to decrease as farms get bigger.

| Exercise 12 | collecting; keying; checking; filing |

Exercise 13
Sample answer

The diagram illustrates a company's application and recruitment process.

Firstly, the people responsible for the vacancy draw up a list of job requirements and these requirements are included in an advertisement, which is placed in a newspaper.

The applicant expresses interest in the job by asking for an application form. The application form is completed and returned by the applicant before a decision is made, whether or not to invite the applicant for an interview. If the candidate is rejected at this stage a letter is sent thanking him/her for the application. The other applicants are invited to attend an interview.

The selected applicants are interviewed and the interviewer decides on a successful applicant and a runner up. The successful candidate is offered the job. If the successful candidate refuses the job then the job is offered to the runner up. Unsuccessful candidates are sent a letter thanking them for attending the interview.

Exercise 14

The following is not relevant

This is not surprising, as it is very difficult to find a good job when you have to use a foreign language. Perhaps the government should offer free language training courses to migrants before they leave their own country.

This could mean that Australian people are lazy or that the migrants have particularly useful skills.

… an overall unemployment rate of 8% is still too high. The government of Victoria must create more jobs so that everyone has a chance to work.

Exercise 15
Sample answer

The table shows the number of foreign language students studying in Australia between 1996 and 1998. The statistics are divided into four groups based on nationality.

Throughout the period by far the largest number of students came from Asia, Asian students making almost 90% of the total. However, the number of Asian students declined from 64 841 in 1996 to 43 220 in 1998, a decrease of around 30%. Consequently the overall number of students also decreased dramatically.

In contrast, the number of Central and South American and African students rose, although they still made up an insignificant proportion of the overall total.

It is interesting to note that the number of European students peaked at 8 012 in 1997 before almost halving to 4 378 in 1998.

To summarise, there was a major decline in the number of international students from 1996 to 1998 This was mainly due to the lower number of Asian students.

Exercise 16
Sample answers

1 The divorce rate will increase steadily over the next 20 years.
2 The average age at marriage will increase.
3 The birth rate will decrease slightly.
4 The exchange rate will go down against the US dollar.
5 There will be a significant population increase.
6 The literacy rate will remain much the same.
7 Pollution in major cities will get worse.
8 There will be a fall in computer prices.
9 The income tax rates will increase.
10 There will be a dramatic rise in life expectancy.
11 The cost of living will rise significantly.
12 The average income will stay much the same.

Exercise 17
Sample answers

Smoking cigarettes should be made illegal.

For: Smoking kills: lung cancer/heart disease.

Passive smoking is also dangerous.

Money spent on health would be much less if no smoking-related diseases.

Immoral to sell a product that is obviously dangerous to user.

Against: Tobacco industry a major source of revenue/jobs/tax.

If illegal create a new black market/more crime/no decrease in people smoking.

People have the right to do things even if it is bad for them.

It is better to be beautiful than rich.

For: Gets you noticed (recent surveys show good-looking people are more likely to get a good job).

Lots of jobs require you to be good-looking.

Makes it easier for you to make friends.

Money does not make you happy, eg Howard Hughes, John Paul Getty.

Against: Money lasts longer than beauty.

Money can buy beauty through cosmetic surgery.

Not necessary to be attractive to be successful, eg male actors such as Danny Devito.

Money guarantees a certain level of comfort and respect.

Shops should be open 24 hours a day.

For: People have less free time so need facilities such as shops available for whenever they are needed.

Businesses should be based on customer needs.

Shopping is now a form of leisure like TV.

Against: Shop workers need holidays as well.

Very few shops offer essential services so don't need to be open all the time.

Society is too commercial as it is.

People do not need to have more opportunity to spend money.

Soon people will be able to shop on the Internet.

People work too long anyway so it's better not to have shops open 24 hours a day.

Shop staff need time with their families too.

Mobile phones are not good for society.

For: Possible radiation.

Increase stress.

There are times when people don't want to be contacted.

Dangerous when driving.

Annoying to other people on the bus or train.

Against: Allow people to be in contact 24 hours a day.

Keeps people in touch with friends and family.

Useful in case of emergency.

People don't need to use vandalised public telephones.

Exercise 18

1 **Reason for writing:** I have lived near Foxley Woods for over forty years and I strongly believe the proposed bypass is not only unnecessary but would destroy the unique character of the area.

2 **Paragraph 2 topic sentence:** Why is there now this sudden need for a new road?

Paragraph 3 topic sentence: Foxley woods is one of this country's few remaining patches of virgin woodland.

3 **Paragraph 2 supporting argument:** Traffic has managed to find it's way through the village of Greystoke with the minimum of delay throughout my life.

Evidence: The other day I carried out an experiment: I drove on the existing road from Blacksheep Dip to Greystoke, a journey of some ten minutes, in exactly four and a half minutes. What is more I made this journey at 5.30 on a Friday afternoon in the so-called rush hour.

Conclusion from evidence: If the existing road is not fast enough, how fast does the council want us to go?

Paragraph 3 supporting argument: It is home to a number of rare species that include Harvey's elephant mouse, the grey headed shrike and the lesser shrew. If the bypass is built these animals will have their habitat disturbed and will run the danger of ending up as road kill. Not only this but new roads bring development, so in all likelihood our woods will soon end up as part of a housing estate.

4   **Action to be taken:** We must stand together and fight this ill begotten barbaric plan.

Exercise 19
Sample plan

A plan might look like this:

Introduction

Effect of international mass media:

Brings people together?

Another advantage

Human rights:

Evidence: Hard to keep abuses secret.

Disadvantages

1   but biased news.

Evidence: Owners of media control the news

2   Media tends to focus on the lowest form of entertainment so everyone can understand it, whatever their culture.

Conclusion: Some advantages but usually aims for the lowest common denominator

Exercise 20

The following is not relevant

Over the past hundred years modern science has advanced faster than ever before. One hundred years ago people were only just starting to use electricity and hadn't discovered antibiotics. Now they have the Internet and will soon be able to clone human beings.

I once saw a film where evil scientists cloned Hitler and tried to take over the world.

Exercise 21

The following is not relevant

It is interesting to note that although Manchester United is popular throughout the world many people in Britain hate them.

Everybody hopes that the Olympics and the world cup will be a great success and that their country will win.

Exercise 22
Sample answers

2   I want to study information technology because it is expanding rapidly so I think it will lead to good jobs.

3   I am planning to study at Dulacca University as it is a leading centre for computer studies.

4   I will have to study several subjects that are all new to me.

5   I am really looking forward to studying although it will be quite difficult.

IELTS practice test: Writing (General Training)

Task 1
Sample answer

Dear Sir/Madam

With reference to your order number 5210.

Last week, I ordered a wardrobe from your mail order company. This was delivered yesterday morning. Unfortunately, on trying to assemble the wardrobe, I discovered that one of the doors was missing. Would it be possible for you to send someone out with a replacement wardrobe one afternoon next week? If you are unable to replace the wardrobe, please send someone to pick it up and refund my credit card for the amount of $225.

Please could you telephone me to let me know when you will be coming, so that I can arrange to be home at this time? Any time after 1.00 pm would be convenient for me, as I work in the morning.

I look forward to hearing from you as soon as possible and to receiving my new wardrobe.

Yours faithfully

Task 2
Sample answer

One of the major problems today is that natural resources such as coal and oil are not renewable and are running out extremely quickly.

It is therefore extremely important that every effort should be made to cut down on the resources used. The most obvious way of doing this is to be more economical. People should be forced to drive smaller cars and cars should be adapted to use petrol as efficiently as possible. Moreover people should be encouraged to use public transport whenever possible. This could be done by taxing cars heavily and using the money to improve the quality of public transport.

Cars are not the only drain on resources. The generation of electricity is also a major problem. Although it has to be admitted that everyone needs electricity, it is often used wastefully. For example are those large neon advertisements in the city centre really necessary? If we really tried everyone could save some electricity by using fewer electrical gadgets and turning off lights when they are not in use.

Energy saving is not enough. In the long term we must find alternative sources of power. The most commonly made suggestion is nuclear power, which generates large amounts of electricity and does not cause major pollution. However, the consequences of a nuclear accident would remain with us for generations and may not be worth the risk. On the other hand clean cheap sources of energy do exist. Solar power, wind power and hydro-electric power have all been suggested as possible solutions.

However, the energy produced is either not enough or not consistent enough to be commercially viable.

It is important that energy is conserved whenever possible, while research into alternative sources of power continues and is perfected.

IELTS practice test: Writing (Academic)

Task 1
Sample answer

The bar chart illustrates the percentage of employees in different occupations absent from work in a given week in 1999.

It is noticeable that the best paying jobs have the lowest rate of absenteeism with managers and administrators recording only around 3.25% absent. This is nearly 1% less than the next lowest rate of absenteeism, which were professional occupations at just over 4%.

On the other hand the highest rate of absenteeism was found in personal and protective occupations, plant and machine operatives and clerical and secretarial jobs. All of these had absent rates of just below 6%, noticeably higher than the rate for all occupations of 4.9%. However, it is also important to notice that the figures show that these sectors employ the highest number of people.

In conclusion, it would seem that managers and administrators are the least likely to be absent from work while plant and machine operators and personal and protective staff are the most likely to call in sick.

Task 2
Sample answer

Most countries encourage consumer spending and consumption as it stimulates economic growth and provides people with jobs. However, many of the products purchased are thrown away after a few months' use. This is a problem when it is remembered that our natural resources are finite.

Human society has developed around the concept of people paying money to buy goods. At the simplest level this is not too much of a problem as people only buy enough to fulfil their basic needs. However, the more advanced the society the more people are encouraged to buy. If people do not replace their clothes or cars every few years with a newer model, manufacturing industries will go bankrupt because of a lack of demand, governments will not be able to support social services and people will lose their jobs. Although this is a fundamental of our society, it is also the cause of many of the problems facing the human race today.

Resources such as the rain forests, oil, coal and natural gas are being used up at an unsustainable rate, while pollution and waste disposal are fast becoming a major problem for the world. Many products have built-in obsolescence, for example cars are only made to last for a few years. This coupled with the advertising world's constant quest for new markets has meant that people's demands have far outstripped their basic needs. This type of economic development may not be sustainable.

Although society relies heavily on consumption, it is vitally important that there is a major shift of attitudes and economies begin to rethink their ideas on economic growth. Consumption needs to be controlled so it has the minimum effect on the environment and the world's resources.